**INSIGHT** **PO**

PROVENCE

Discovery CHANNEL

APA PUBLICATIONS
Part of the Langenscheidt Publishing Group L

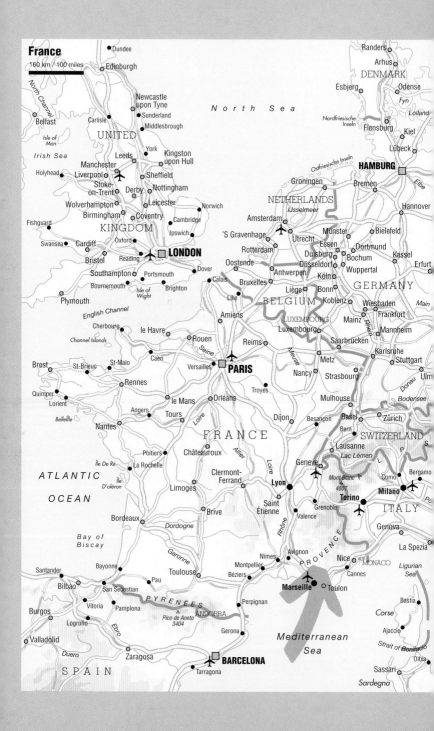

Welcome!

This is one of 133 itinerary-based Pocket Guides produced by the editors of Insight Guides, whose books have set the standard for visual travel guides since 1970. With top-quality photography and authoritative recommendations, this guidebook is designed to help visitors get the most out of the city and its surroundings during a short stay. To this end, Insight's expert on the region, Mark Fincham, has devised 13 routes.

The guide begins at the foot of Mont-Ventoux with a tour around the Dentelles de Montmirail. It then heads south to Avignon, an ancient Rhône staging post and erstwhile home to the popes, from where it is a short hop to Arles. From there you can head to sophisticated Aix-en-Provence and then to the coast, to Cassis, the Ile de Porquerolles and St-Tropez. Our correspondent then turns inland again to explore the Var and the Luberon. The guide also includes an introduction to the history of the area, plus a section packed with practical tips and restaurant and hotel recommendations.

 Mark Fincham first went to live in Provence in the summer of 1982, when he enjoyed long hot days of idleness and pleasure. At the time he did not think he had been especially smitten, but when summer came round again he thought only of Provence. Then he found himself arriving for the *réveillon*, the celebration of the New Year when the skies are blown clear by the mistral. Soon he was coming for Easter and then for the *vendange* (grape harvest). Finally he bowed to the inevitable and moved to the region.

C O N T E N T S

Pages 2/3: Roussillon in the Luberon

Shopping and Eating Out

Tips on what to buy and where to eat. Includes a detailed menu decoder **66–77**

Calendar of Events

What to watch out for in a year in Provence..........**78**

Practical Information

All the essential background information for your visit to Provence, including a discriminating list of hotels **80–91**

Maps

Pages 8/9: the harbour at Cassis

Index and Credits 92–94

HISTORY

In his book on Provence, Ford Madox Ford described the region as 'a highway along which travelled continuously the stream of the arts, of thought, of the traditions of life'. The process he so aptly describes has created what could be identified as the supreme type of Mediterranean culture. The presiding genius is, of course, that great gift, the sun. Its characteristic features are the products of the olive and grape, the universal cafés, the *cours* and *boulevards* where people meet and talk, the customary evening promenade, an *apéritif* and a game of *boules*, the love of running water expressed in the ubiquitous fountains, the many social and cultural manifestations

The Greeks first introduced the vine

such as village fêtes, markets, concerts and theatre and, in winter, the devotion to *la chasse* (the hunt). In this brief history I hope to show how all this came about.

The Greeks

The Greeks who came to Provence in 600BC are attributed with introducing the techniques for cultivating vines. Today vineyards cover about 65,000 hectares (250 sq. miles) of land, a sizeable chunk

CULTURE

of the region. They are the chief characteristic of the Provençal countryside, and their wines are found on every table. The other gift of the Greeks was the olive tree. Though less extensive than the vine, it has nevertheless contributed to another of the definitive characteristics of Provençal culture – a cuisine based on olive oil (as opposed to butter).

The overriding dominance of the vine in the Provençal countryside has been steadily reduced over the last 50 years, as irrigation schemes have enabled intensive cultivation of fruits and vegetables less suited to dry conditions. These schemes include the taming of the Durance and Verdon rivers by building dams at Serre-Ponçon and Sainte-Croix, and the creation of Le Canal de Provence which feeds a 3,000-km (1,850-mile) system of irrigation canals. Greenhouse production is now also widespread. Thanks to the intensive cultivation of peaches, apples and sunflowers, Provence is France's leading producer of fruit and vegetables, and a major centre for the food-processing industry.

The Romans

The Romans founded their first settlement in Provence in 122BC after their victory over the indigenous tribes, variously described as Franks or Gauls. The site, named Aquae Sextiae, would eventually become Aix-en-Provence. This was the beginning of Roman rule in Provence and it lasted until the fall of the Roman Empire in AD476. Curiously, the Romans had originally come to Provence to

Roman ruins at St-Rémy

help their traditional allies, the Greeks, whose trading ambitions were hindered by the Gauls. However, they increasingly began to see Provence as a stepping-stone between Italy and Spain, the spoil of their victory over the Carthaginians. They also liked what they found and named it *Provincia* – the Roman province. In 103BC the Roman general Marius consolidated Rome's hold on the area by defeating a huge army of Teutons from northern Europe. The name Marius has lived on in the common memory and until recently was a common boy's name in Provence.

Unlike the Greeks, who came to Provence to trade, the Romans were true imperialists. The whole cultural apparatus of Rome was imposed on the new province. Towns were built according to the Roman urban plan and each one had its own individual forum, arena, theatre, public baths and fountains, and three great roads were constructed to link them – the Aurelian Way, the Agrippan Way and the Domitian Way.

Vestiges of this titanic building programme can be seen all over Provence, in small bridges and ruins and often in antique remains incorporated into the walls of contemporary buildings, as in the Nord-Pinus Hotel in Arles. Then there are the mighty public buildings of Fréjus, Arles, Nîmes, Orange and Vaison. This heritage has profoundly influenced the shape of present-day Provence. The central *cours* or *place* and the fountain of every town and village are derived from the Roman forum. In Aix-en-Provence these fountains are the Roman signature on a town that at first sight bears little imprint of its Roman history, since they are animated by the thermal springs, the *aquae* after which Sextius named this site.

The great Roman arenas of Fréjus, Arles, Nîmes and Orange are a graphic illustration of the way in which Provence has absorbed and adapted its past. One moment they are mute witnesses to Provençal history, the next a vital part of contemporary cultural life, as venues for concerts and bullfights. At the moment when the matador is lining up for the kill and the crowd quietens in anticipation it is almost impossible to imagine that the arena ever existed for any other purpose.

The Christians

Christianity, no less than the Greeks or the Romans, left its imprint on the complex grid of Provençal history. From the legendary conversion of Provence to Christianity in the 1st century,

Early representations of Christ

after the miraculous landing of the boat from Judea – the so-called Boat of Bethany – bearing amongst others, Lazarus, Mary Magdalene and Martha, religion has exerted a strong influence.

Monasticism took an early hold and in the 12th century the Cistercians built the great Romanesque abbeys of Sénanque, Silvacane and Thoronet. Perhaps not surprisingly the heavy, simple forms of the Romanesque – with their reminder of classical shapes – struck a chord in Provence, unleashing an intense period of building activity. Romanesque churches from this period are a distinctive feature of many Provençal villages.

Provence was also a destination for pilgrims who came to the superb Gothic basilica of St Maximin, which stands on the spot where, according to legend, Mary Magdalene was buried. The papacy came to Avignon in the 14th century putting Provence, for a short while, at the centre of the Christian world. Though the popes returned to Rome in 1377, they retained control of an area known

as the *Comtat Venaissin* (today the department of the Vaucluse) and their influence and the magnificent legacy of their building continued to inform the life of this area, notably in the Religious Wars of the 16th century when many Protestant villages in the Luberon were destroyed.

Though religious observance has declined, the Christian history of Provence still influences the *fêtes* that are part of the cultural life of every village. Some are clearly part of the Christian tradition, such as those on Christmas Eve, when the Nativity is enacted by members of the village (one of the best known of these is in the village of Séguret in the Vaucluse). This is itself an extension of the popular Provençal custom of decorating a crib with

The Romanesque church at Gigondas

santons – clay figures representing the cast of the Nativity. Collections of these figures are found in all the regional museums devoted to popular culture and are considered typically Provençal. However, this practice was actually imported from Italy in the 16th century and rapidly incorporated into Provençal culture.

'Houses in Provence' by Cézanne, who was born in Aix-en-Provence

In many cases the Christian foundations of a *fête* have been forgotten or overlayed with a new meaning and the *fête* has become a popular celebration. One such is the rowdy *Bravade* of 16 May in St-Tropez celebrating the naming of the town after the Roman martyr Torpes (Tropez), who was decapitated after converting to Christianity and washed up in the one-time fishing port that now bears his name. More famous is the *Fête et pélerinage* to Saintes-Maries-de-la-Mer. The 700-year-old annual pilgrimage to the town where the Boat of Bethany landed is now famous as a two-day festival of the gypsies. Their patron saint is Sarah, the slave of the Marys (Magdalene, Salomé and Jacobé) who arrived in the boat.

A New Breed of Visitor

In 1763 the English writer Tobias Smollett travelled to the South of France in search of a climate that might restore his health. Although Smollett did not find his trip an agreeable experience, the published account of his travels brought the climate of the south, particularly the crisp, dry winters, to the attention of a larger public. He wrote, 'There is less rain and wind at Nice than in any other part of the world that I know… [the] air being dry, pure, heavy, and elastic, must be agreeable to the constitution of those who labour under disorders, arising from weak nerves, obstructed perspiration… a viscidity of lymph, and a languid circulation.' Since this described a broad variety of disorders Smollett was soon followed by coach-loads of invalids, and also by the English aristocracy, who took to wintering on the Riviera to escape the damp and cold of England.

For these first tourists the season lasted only from November to March. The summer was considered hot and unhealthy until the 1920s, when a few daring Americans persuaded one hotel owner to remain open in the summer.

The French were generally less excited by the discovery of the South of France, though they established resorts in Hyères and St-Raphael. The introduction of the paid holiday in 1936 – two weeks statutory minimum – changed all that, and they too began flocking to the south, many of them in order to see the sea for the first time.

A parallel development was a migration of artists and writers to the South of France. The artists were attracted by the clarity of the Mediterranean light and the writers drawn by the cheap living conditions. The first artists whose work publicised the area and shaped people's perceptions of it were the painters Vincent Van Gogh, Paul Cézanne and Paul Signac. A number of writers were also influential, including Colette, F. Scott Fitzgerald, Somerset Maugham and Françoise Sagan, who all published books set in Provence. They contributed to a rising tide of publicity that created the image of a warm Mediterranean paradise and helped establish the reputation of Provence as the place for those interested in the arts.

All this publicity was as nothing compared to the tumult that was unleashed by one *artiste* at the end of the 1950s. Her name was Brigitte Bardot and the scenes of her making love and swimming naked at St-Tropez in the film *And God Created Woman*, brought St-Tropez and Provence to the notice of the world, and brought the world to St-Tropez and Provence.

Year-round sun brought tourism

By 2004 the annual number of visitors to Provence and the Riviera had reached 34 million, attracted by the glamour, the 2,500 hours of sunshine per year and the rich cultural environment. Today tourism is one of the primary industries in Provence: visitors spend some €10 billion per year and provide 86,000 jobs.

The Provençals

What are the people like who preside over all this? Since antiquity Provence has lain on one of the great highways of Europe and the region has consequently assimilated many different peoples of the Mediterranean. In the Arles region, the influence of Spain can be seen in the people and their local customs, most obviously in the bullfight; the last major influx of Spaniards were refugees from the Spanish Civil War. In the coastal region around Marseilles the people are still said to bear the imprint of their Greek heritage. And in the Var and the area surrounding Nice the influence of Italy can be clearly seen. Nice was an Italian possession for centuries and received, along with the Var, a large influx of Italians at the end of the 19th century. Since 1950 the south of France has received many settlers from Algeria, Tunisia and Morocco. They have been accommodated rather less smoothly than the earlier settlers but their influence is certainly reflected, for example, in the cuisine of this part of Provence.

These influxes have made for an open society, where the foreigner is generally made to feel welcome. Most Provençals are friendly to visitors and they enjoy contact with other people, particularly if this leads to a large general discussion. Their philosophy is live and let live. Paradoxically, however, this does not always extend to their own countrymen.

This attitude can be traced deep in the history of Provence, a history of separation and independence from the rest of France. Politically it was not joined to the kingdom of France until 1481. Culturally its links were with the Mediterranean countries. French did not replace Provençal as the official language of Provence until 1539. The papal court in Avignon conducted its affairs in Latin and Provençal – known as the *langue d'oc*. As Provence came increasingly under the sway of the centralising and unifying power of the state in the 19th century, a movement arose called the *Félibrige*, whose essential aim was to assert and preserve its cultural independence, including the revival of interest in the *langue d'oc*.

One of the best reasons for visiting Provence

Historical Highlights

600BC Greek traders found the port of Marseille, bringing the olive tree and the vine with them to Provence.

122 Foundation of Aquae-Sextiae (Aix-en-Provence) by the Romans.

103 The Roman general Marius defeats the Teutons.

58–51 Subjugation of Gaul by Julius Caesar. Romans impose imperial rule on their new province.

19 Building of the Pont du Gard, which still exists today.

12 Romans occupy the settlement at Vaison.

AD46 The Boat of Bethany lands at Saintes-Maries-de-la-Mer.

476 Fall of the Roman Empire.

500 Vaison is invaded by the Burgundians.

536 Provence comes under the rule of the Franks.

1032 Provence is annexed to the Holy Roman Empire.

1125 The flowering of Troubador poetry and the Courts of Love, exemplified in Les Baux.

1152 Consecration of the church of St-Trophime.

1160 Foundation of the abbey of Sénanque.

1309 Clement V, a Frenchman, is given the papal crown.

1316 Pope John XXII establishes the papacy in Avignon.

1388 The eastern part of Provence, known as the County of Nice, comes under the rule of the House of Savoy (Italy).

1409 University of Aix is founded.

1481 Provence is joined to the kingdom of France.

1539 French replaces Provençal, the *langue d'oc*, as the official language.

1545 Destruction of Protestant villages in the Luberon during the Wars of Religion.

1763 English writer Tobias Smollett travels through the South of France; his writing attracted the first tourists – even though it wasn't entirely complimentary.

1789 The French Revolution.

1790 Provence is divided into three *départements*: Basse-Alpes, Bouches-du-Rhône and Var.

1815 The end of the Napoleonic Wars; the English aristocracy begins to winter in the south of France.

1839 Cézanne is born in Aix.

1854 Founding of the *Félibrige*.

1855 Paris–Avignon railway built.

1860 The County of Nice is returned to France.

1865 Nice is linked by rail to Marseille and the valley of the Rhône.

1869 Publication of Daudet's *Lettres de Mon Moulin*.

1887 The term Côte d'Azur is coined.

1888 Van Gogh settles in Arles.

1892 The pontillist painter, Paul Signac, settles in St-Tropez.

1923 Regulations for the production of wines in Châteauneuf-du-Pape are introduced.

1925 The writer Colette moves to St-Tropez.

1936 Introduction of the paid holiday in France.

1941 Bandol receives *appellation contrôlée* status.

1944 The Allies land on the beaches of Pampelonne towards the end of World War II.

1960 Serre-Ponçon dam opens.

1960 Brigitte Bardot hits St-Tropez, starring in the film *And God Created Woman*.

1970 A6–A7 motorway, the *autoroute du soleil*, links Paris and the South.

1975 The Sainte-Croix dam opens.

1976 Completion of *Le Canal de Provence*.

1981 The TGV (*Train à Grande Vitesse*) links Paris and Nice.

1992 Catastrophic flooding in Provence.

1998 The Front National attracts 27 percent of votes in the region.

2001 The Paris to Marseille TGV link opens.

2005 France wins the bid for the International Thermonuclear Experimental Reactor (ITER), to be built at Cadarache in the Luberon.

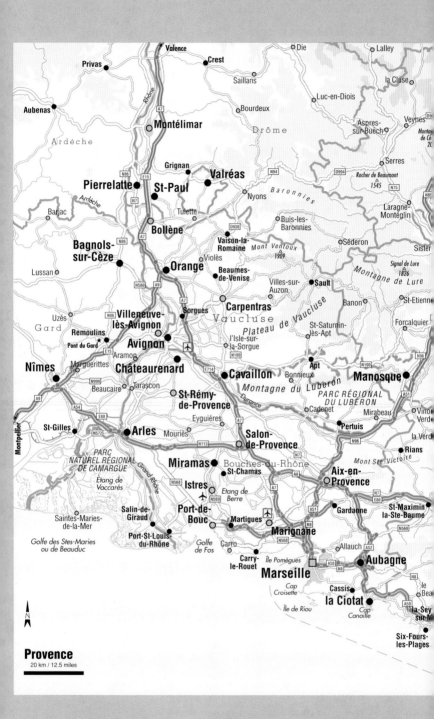

Provence

20 km / 12.5 miles

Day Itiner

The southeast corner of France is known as Provence-Alpes-Côte d'Azur and is divided into six *départements*, Alpes-de-Haute-Provence, Hautes-Alpes, Alpes-Maritimes, Bouches-du-Rhône, Var and Vaucluse. However, the boundaries of the 'real' Provence, like the ingredients of the 'real' *bouillabaisse*, are a subject of dispute.

The area covered by this guide is contained within the *départements* of the Vaucluse, Bouches-du-Rhône and Var. A car is highly recommended for these itineraries, although any one of them could be achieved in a day by a good touring cyclist. The routes describe an uneven circle, starting in the north at the foot of Mont-Ventoux, heading south towards the coast, moving along the coast, then heading inland and finally back west towards Mont-Ventoux. Places to stay are recommended in the *Practical Information* section (*see pages 84–8)*, with a price guide.

Most of the tours would benefit from starting before 9.30am, before the day really has a chance to warm up. The tours are also shaped by the desirability of eating at lunchtime. This makes sense for several reasons: it is a good time to stop and absorb the morning's sights, and avoid walking around in the midday heat when everything closes down. Furthermore, in France the main meal of the day is often lunch, and is usually served from noon until 2pm.

Suggestions as to what to do during between 2pm and 5pm, when the sun can really burn, are also provided. As the ideal solution – taking a siesta – is not always an option, I have tried to ensure that by this time of the day the itinerary will take you either into the countryside, where there should be shade, or near water. A range of places to stay is included in the *Accommodation* section beginning on page 84.

Preceding pages: Provence has a long tradition of artists. Below: ready to go

The Dentelles de Montmirail

1. Picturesque Provence

A circuit of the Dentelles de Montmirail, taking in Roman ruins, medieval towns, perched villages, 'santons', the sumptuous fruity wines of Gigondas and the decadent sweet wines of Beaumes-de-Venise. 63 km (39 miles).

The **Dentelles de Montmirail** is a chain of mountains extending over about 15km (9 miles) of the **Vaucluse**, a *département* of great natural beauty known in France for the quality of its fresh fruit and vegetables. I would recommend **Bédoin**, nestling in the sunny pastures at the foot of the Mont-Ventoux, as an ideal base. Begin the day at the *Office du Tourisme*, where the *accueil* (welcome) is always warm and they are generous with local maps and guides.

The D19 from Bédoin to **Malaucène** snakes between the Dentelles and the lower slopes of Mont-Ventoux, with soaring mountain scenery opening out on all sides. The fortress-like south front of the parish church of St-Michael greets you as you enter Malaucène; in summer the people of the town like to sit on the cool stone bench at the base of this wall. As the gateway to the Alpine north face of the Mont-Ventoux, Malaucène is a busy town, but time can be better spent at our main morning destination, **Vaison-la-Romaine**.

The D938 leaves Malaucène in the shade of a long avenue of trees and before long the medieval quarter of Vaison comes into view,

The fortified medieval village of Vaison-la-Romaine

hanging precariously over the road. Cross the Roman bridge that was seriously damaged by floods in 1992 but has since been restored, and leave your car in the large space in the town centre. From here Vaison is easily explored on foot.

The town splits into two distinct parts, separated by the River Ouvèze. On one side are the Roman and present-day towns, on the other the medieval town and traces of an earlier Celtic occupation. The main Roman site known as the **Quartier de Puymin** (entrance opposite the Tourist Office) with a museum, ancient theatre and large villa is magnificent and should not be missed. It is in my view far more impressive than the celebrated Roman site at Glanum just outside St-Rémy. Contemporary accounts described it as the *urbs opulentissima* and one can imagine this was justified. One ticket gives admission to the Roman ruins, the on-site museum and the cloisters of the town's cathedral, **Notre-Dame-de-Nazareth**. The opening times are the same for all sites (closed Tuesday). For further information, call the tourist office on 04 90 36 02 11.

A five-minute walk down the Grand' Rue and back across the Roman bridge brings you to the heavily fortified medieval village surmounted by its ruined castle. The maze of streets contains a number of craft shops and interesting 17th-century townhouses. The lanes are rewarding to explore, but first turn left past the fountain under the Porte Vieille-Rue de l'Horloge and follow Rue de l'Eglise past a fine row of cottages until you come to a small square in front of the church, from where there is an excellent view. From here Rue de Charité leads up to the ruined castle.

Back in the main town Place Montfort — swamped by a market on Tuesday — is lined by *brasseries* on one side and is a good place to have a beer or perhaps a cup of

Well-proportioned Roman, Vaison

tea in the **Café des Arts**, an old-fashioned café on the corner of the square. Afterwards, for all but the most ardent fan of Roman history, it is probably time to leave Vaison.

The next place on this itinerary is **Séguret**. Leave Vaison on the D977 (direction Carpentras) and after 5km (3 miles) turn off onto the D88 (direction Séguret). The exits from Vaison are not entirely clear and if you find yourself on the D975, direction Orange, don't worry – continue to Roaix, take the D7 on your left, which crosses the River Ouvèze, and go straight across the D977 onto the D88 to Séguret. This is what the French call a *route du vin*, literally a wine-road, and you will see on all sides the vines belonging to the area designated Côte du Rhône Villages, of which Séguret is one.

As a general rule, the wines from these villages will be of a higher quality than a wine that is designated simply Côte du Rhône.

Séguret has two superb restaurants, **Le Mesclun** *(see page 73)* and **La Table du Comtat** *(see page 84)*, and it is difficult to choose between them. La Table du Comtat is also a small hotel and is therefore smarter and a little more expensive; the owner-chef is a member of the exclusive *Maître Cuisinier de France* order and his cooking has a high reputation. Le Mesclun offers a new menu for each season, and for €25 you can eat exceptionally well. If you arrive too late for lunch, you can find a snack at **L'Eglantine**, a charming *salon de thé*.

Seasonal produce is his business

Having said all this, to eat lunch is not the only reason to come to Séguret. Its aspect overlooking the Plain of Orange is glorious. The village, which is designated as a national monument, has a 12th-century church, 14th-century belfry and a superb 17th-century fountain. It is further celebrated for its Nativity play on Christmas Eve. The parts are filled by villagers and handed down through families. This is a variation on the traditional crèche peopled by symbolic clay figures called *santons*, a feature of Christmas in Provence.

These figures can all be seen in **L'Oustau Dei Santoun** of Jean-Louis Romère, near the top of the village past the Cellier des Vignerons. His atelier contains *santons* from the two greatest masters of the craft, Paul Fouque of Aix-en-Provence and Marcel Carbonel of Marseille. He will be happy to show you the different styles of *santons* and discuss their history.

Jean-Louis wears another hat as a wine-maker, and you should not leave without a bottle or two of his extraordinary red wine, made in traditional style from very old vines. It is a real *vin de garde* (a wine to keep).

Below this 'balcony' town, as it is sometimes called, you can see the town of Sablet, whose streets are built in concentric circles around the church in a fashion that is typically Provençal. Sablet has many picturesque streets and an excellent *caveau des vignerons*, where you can taste all the local wines.

The next stop is the celebrated wine town of Gigondas, just a few more kilometres along the D7. Wine enthusiasts should look out for a left turn about halfway between Sablet and Gigondas and the

The wines of Beaumes-de-Venise are sweet

sign for Domaine les Pallières. Once owned by the Roux Brothers, this estate has now been bought by the renowned Brunier family, who also own the Vieux Télégraphe vineyard in Châteauneuf-du-Pape. Their estate is perfectly situated in the foothills of the Dentelles and makes one of the best wines of the *appellation*. You can no longer visit for tastings, but the wine is on sale at the Caveau de Gigondas *(see below)*.

The best Gigondas are dense, ruby-coloured wines loaded with fruit and alcohol and, although some producers will advise you to keep them for up to 10 years, they can also be drunk immediately, an irresistible reason for buying a few bottles while you're here.

Gigondas is the Vauclusian equivalent of the one-horse town: its

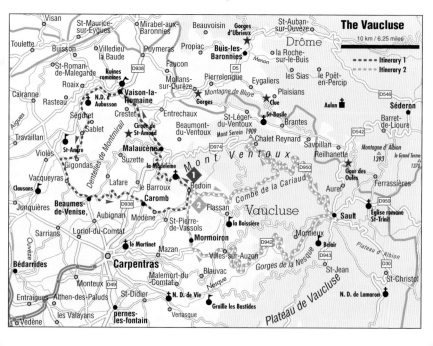

horse is the vine, stabled in the Caveau de Gigondas in the Place du Portail, where you can taste and buy the wines of all the local producers. The red wines labelled Côtes du Rhône Villages also merit attention. Those from the Gigondas estate of Les Goubert are highly recommended.

The village is dominated by its church and the vestiges of the château constructed in the 14th century by the counts of Orange. Wind your way through the old streets to the terrace of the church for another great panorama. Gigondas is a starting point for many walks in the Dentelles, and though these may have to wait for another day, you could take your car up to the orientation point of the Col du Cayron (396m/1,300ft), facing the mountain peaks, for a memorable view.

Over the ridge is **Beaumes-de-Venise**, only a 10-minute drive by way of the D7 (direction Carpentras) and the D81, which branches off to the left after about 6km (4 miles). Sheltered from the mistral at the foot of the Durban Plateau, the town is chiefly famous for its decadently sweet wine, the Muscat de Beaumes-de-Venise. The muscat grapes grown on the super-warm south-facing slopes attain a heady degree of alcohol and seem to soak up the aromas of the apricots and peaches that load the trees in summer. This heady nectar is taken locally as an *apéritif*, a habit frowned on by purists who believe that it should be exclusively a dessert wine.

Domaine de Durban makes one of the best Muscats and the twisting climb up to this estate (take the D21 out of the town, turn left immediately onto route de Lafare, turn left again where you will see signs to the estate) reveals another face of the Dentelles – now steep, terraced slopes looking like the green foothills of the Andes. It is appropriate to finish the day with a glass of sweet wine in your hand and the Dentelles spread out before you.

Leaving Beaumes-de-Venise it is just a short drive back to Bédoin, via Caromb, which is where tomorrow's itinerary begins.

Santons, Provence's traditional Christmas figures

2. Mont-Ventoux

A visit to Mont-Ventoux, followed by a tour through the glorious gorges of the Nesque valley, plus lunch and shopping for lavender and nougat in the village of Sault.

If your schedule enables you to spend another day in the Vaucluse, try this tour, which takes you to Mont-Ventoux, the *géant* (giant) of Provence, around which many myths and stories have accumulated. The climb from the base of the mountain to the summit at 1,909m (6,233ft) leads you from a Mediterranean to an Alpine landscape, through many transitions of temperature and vegetation.

The first recorded ascent of the mountain was that of the Italian poet Petrarch. He spent part of his childhood in Carpentras and later lived in Avignon. In 1327 he scrambled up the steep slopes in the company of his brother. If you have the time and the energy this is undoubtedly the best way to tackle Mont-Ventoux (detailed hiking guides to the various routes can be purchased at the local Tourist Office in Bédoin).

The Ventoux is frequently included as one of the stages in the Tour de France cyle race and it was on these steep slopes that the English rider Tom Simpson died in 1967. This ascent is without doubt the ultimate challenge for a cyclist, since the steep slope is unremitting and singularly unrelieved by bends.

If cycling isn't your cup of tea, and the infamous Provençal heat is getting you down, do not despair, for the summit can also be reached by car. From Bédoin, you need to take the D974 (direction Chalet Reynard, the base of one of the Ventoux's popular winter ski-stations). The mountain's summit is a further 6km (4 miles) from here.

Though this area, which is known as *l'aire royale du vent et du ciel* (the royal place of wind and sky), is basically rather a mess, you should hardly notice this, since the view is second to none. During the summer the landscape below can be lost in a heat haze and a good case can be made for going up the mountain when the mistral is blowing the skies clear. Of course these weather

Mont-Ventoux features in the Tour de France

André Boyer and his nougat

conditions have their own
perils, notably a considerably lower temperature than down below, and a wind that threatens to toss you
back to Bédoin whence you came.

Descending from the summit you can reach Bédoin in a circuit
via Malaucène. However, it is much better (even though it might take
you more time) to return the way you came to Chalet Reynard.
From there, take the D164 (direction **Sault**) and descend through the
beautiful but little-known gorges
of the Nesque.

Typically Provençal

These deep valleys number
among Provence's most outstanding natural features. If your schedule allows, stop for a while in
Sault to visit the shop of André
Boyer Maître Nougatier. His
delicious nougat is made from a
combination of local almonds and
aromatic lavender honey, a speciality of the region.

The **Bar de la Promenade**,
which is located at the south end
of the village *promenade* overlooking the plains is the place in
Sault for a drink and a good cheap
lunch. During late June and early
July the plains are covered in
beautiful purple lavender, which
makes for a delightful view.

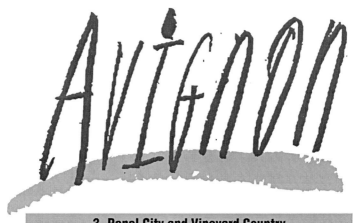

3. Papal City and Vineyard Country

This full day's tour begins and ends in Avignon; the morning includes a visit to the Palais des Papes (Popes' Palace), the Rocher des Doms garden and a walk along the ramparts. Leaving around noon, head for Châteauneuf-du-Pape for a good lunch and numerous wine tastings. From there go to the Pont du Gard, take a kayak down the River Gardon and then return to Avignon for a promenade and supper. 80km (50 miles).

If you are coming to Avignon by car, plan to arrive early (by 9am in the summer) and park in one of the free parking areas just outside the city walls. The most convenient are the areas by the Porte du Rhône (for visiting the palaces) or at the other end of the city, the Porte de la République, opposite the station. If there is no room in these areas, you can also park (for a fee) in one of the parking lots that ring the old city. The area within the walls is small and easily explored on foot; taking a car inside is unnecessary and parking almost impossible. For the out-of-town (afternoon) part of this itinerary, pack swimwear.

The town of Avignon occupies a rocky site at the strategic confluence of the Rhône and Durance rivers. The Romans marched past it on the Agrippan Way, following the Rhône valley from Arles to Lyon; later, travellers coming south would take a boat from Lyon to Avignon. The most celebrated arrival was

Avignon from Pont St-Bénézet

30

Entertainment in Place de l'Horloge

that of Pope John XXII who installed himself in Avignon in 1316, placing the town in the full stream of European culture. Although the last pope left Avignon in 1377, the papal legacy is ever present in the city's palaces and vibrant cultural life.

There is an old Provençal proverb that goes: '*Qui s'éloigne d'Avignon perd la raison*,' meaning 'He who leaves Avignon has lost his reason.' This is rather similar to the British saying, 'He who is tired of London is tired of life', and, like London, Avignon is a city that inspires both love and hatred. Petrarch thought the city 'The thoroughfare of vice, the sewers of the earth.' We may have to allow for a little Italian bias here, but by all accounts Avignon had its dark side then and still does. John Evelyn, the English diarist who wrote an account of his travels through Europe in the 17th century, was much impressed with Avignon: 'The walls of the Citty (being all square huge free stone) are absolutely the most neate and best repaire that in my life I ever saw: it is full of well built Palaces.'

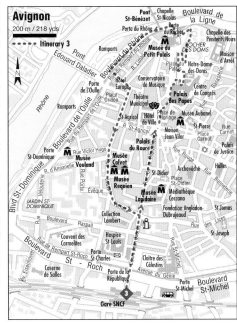

The key to liking Avignon today, especially when coming to the city from the languorous countryside, is to be aware that in the summer it seethes with people and heat, reaching a climax

From the Palais des Papes

during the **Avignon Theatre Festival** (usually the last two weeks of July and the first week of August). The streets are animated day and night by street performers, musicians and young actors handing out flyers for their shows. In my view, it is a time to visit but not to stay, unless you love the theatre. Spring and early summer are lovely, when the town comes to life after winter, during which the mistral howls through the city, driving street life inside.

Avignon has a north–south axis running from the ramparts of the Palais des Papes, through the Place de l'Horloge, to the Porte de la République at the southern end. The **Place de l'Horloge** is the heart of the city; centre of café life and a popular breakfast spot, it is our first rendez-vous. From the Porte de la République it is a 10-minute walk along the Cours J Jaurès and Rue de la République. Stop at the **Tourist Office** to pick up maps and guides.

The main site in Avignon is the monumental **Palais des Papes** (open daily; guided tours and visits with audio guide in several languages; admission fee; tel: 04 90 27 50 00). I can add nothing to the already copious literature on the architecture and history of the palace but I should warn you that you will walk through a

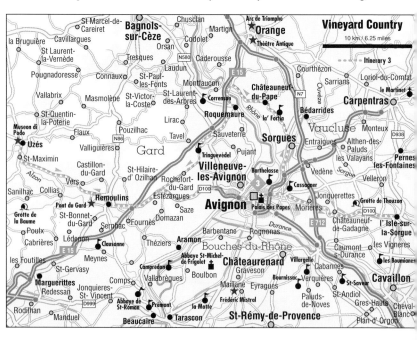

succession of empty rooms; only the magnificent friezes and frescos bear witness to the former decorative splendour. It requires a leap of imagination to picture the sumptuous luxury that surrounded the popes. Perhaps the sheer scale of everything is the giveaway; the shopping list for the coronation banquet of Pope Clement VI included: 118 cattle, 1,023 sheep, 101 calves, 914 young goats, 60 pigs, 69 quintals of bacon (a quintal=100kg or 2,200lbs), 1,500 capons, 3,043 hens, 7,428 chickens, 1,195 geese, 50,000 tarts, 6 quintals of almonds, 2 quintals of sugar, 39,980 eggs and 95,000 loaves of bread. The kitchens are suitably large. Adjacent is the magnificent art collection of the **Petit Palais**, a wealth of medieval paintings and sculptures (closed Tuesday; admission fee; tel: 04 90 86 44 58).

Vines and remains at Châteauneuf

Leaving the palace walk away from the Place de l'Horloge past the cathedral and go up into the **Rocher des Doms garden**, where you can recover your sense of proportion and admire the view of the Rhône and the **Pont St-Bénézet** – made famous by the song *Sur le Pont d'Avignon*. The bridge is a favourite spot for watching the sun set (open daily; admission fee; tel: 04 90 27 51 07).

Avignon has a number of good museums, but one that should not be missed is the **Musée Calvet** (65 Rue Joseph Vernet; closed Tuesday; admission fee; tel: 04 90 86 33 84), a lovely colonnaded building full of tapestries, sculptures, and French paintings of the 18th–20th centuries. You can see the only painting by Van Gogh in Provence, *Les Wagons du Chemin de Fer*, at the **Musée Angladon** (5 Rue Laboureur; May–October closed Monday, November–April closed Monday and Tuesday; admission fee; tel: 04 90 82 29 03).

West of Place de l'Horloge are the more expensive shops selling furniture, clothing, jewellery, with markets and larger stores to the east. For the moment, however, postpone ideas of shopping, locate the car and set off on the road to **Châteauneuf-du-Pape**.

Once on the ring road, follow signs for Orange and Carpentras. At the first major junction take the left filter onto the N7 (direction Sorgues and Orange). The road crosses the River Ouvèze and shortly afterwards you will see the D17, the first turning for Châteauneuf. I prefer to ignore the D17 and go on to the D192, for this road winds through a small plain of vineyards to the east, slowly revealing Châteauneuf in the distance. There is a car park on the right just before the post office as you enter the town. From

Pont du Gard

here it is a short walk up the hill to the **Place de la Fontaine**, the centre of the village.

The history of Châteauneuf is indissolubly linked with that of Avignon and the 14th-century popes. The château looming over the village, greatly damaged during World War II, was built by the popes as a retreat and summer residence.

The popes are also credited with stirring wider interest in the wines of Châteauneuf. In his story *La Mule du Pape* in *Lettres de Mon Moulin*, Alphonse Daudet wrote of the Avignon pope who every Sunday after vespers rode 12km (7.5 miles) out to the plain around Châteauneuf to survey the progress of the vines he had planted himself and would pass the afternoon in the sun drinking a bottle of local wine – 'that excellent wine, the colour of rubies, which from then on would be called the Châteauneuf-du-Pape'. There are around 120 producers of this wine variety and most of them have a *cave* in the village or its environs.

Mule-du-Pape *(see page 74)*, a restaurant on Place de la Fontaine is a Châteauneuf institution. Family cooking (such as *aïoli* and *soupe au pistou*) is the order of the day at the brasserie downstairs (the restaurant upstairs is reserved for large groups).

After lunch there are a number of options: a walk up to the château, a *dégustation* (wine tasting) or a visit to the interesting wine museum on the premises of the Maison Brotte. If this is not to your taste, there is a swimming pool open in summer near the car park.

Not much later than 3pm you should turn your thoughts to the magnificent **Pont du Gard**. The journey is about 35km (20 miles), leaving on the D17 (direction Orange), and then turning left onto the D976 (direction Roquemaure). Continue in the direction of Remoulins, from where the Pont du Gard is signposted. You are now in the *département* of the Gard, which lies outside the present-day boundaries of the politico-economic region of Provence. However, for the purposes of this guide, it can be argued that the Pont du Gard, as a great Roman construction, is within the context of a larger notion of Provence; certainly it would be a shame to miss it.

The Pont du Gard is an aqueduct spanning the River Gardon. It is the only substantial remains of a system built to carry water the 50km (30 miles) to Nîmes from a spring near Uzès; it has been calculated that its daily flow was somewhere around 200 million litres (44 million gallons). To me this is an extraordinary tribute to the quality of Roman civilisation.

To see the Pont in the conventional mannner, follow the signs to the car park and walk up. A bridge added in the 18th century enables you to cross the river on foot under the aqueduct. This in itself is impressive. You can also scramble up the hill to the top of the aqueduct; you could once walk across, as the channel was covered to keep the water clean, but this is no longer possible. The Pont du Gard now has a huge visitors' centre, with displays, exhibitions and films on the history and construction of the aqueduct, as well as a children's activity centre (open daily; admission fee for visitors' centre, aqueduct is free; tel: 08 20 90 33 30).

Alternatively you could view the acqueduct from a kayak. These can be picked up at Collias – ignore signs for the Pont du Gard and continue on the D981 until you reach the D112 (direction Collias); just before Collias turn left down a narrow lane to the river following signs to **Kayak Vert**. The trip downstream takes about 90 minutes; allow half an hour to get back to the car. Kayak Vert have a courtesy bus from a point just below the bridge. There is no finer or more appropriate way to see the Pont du Gard – built by the Romans to satisfy their vast appetite and love for water – than from the water itself, floating round a bend in the river.

The return to Avignon is quickly done, via Remoulins and the N100 to Villeneuve-les-Avignon. If you have any energy left this is the time to do some shopping.

If you have an extra day in Avignon and it happens to be a Saturday or Sunday, you are within easy reach of two of the best markets in Provence. On Saturday the lovely town of **Uzès** is buried under piles of fresh produce, olive oils, soaps and fabrics, and hums with activity (leave Avignon as though returning to the Pont du Gard and continue on the D981 to Uzès). Sunday is the day to visit the famous antique and flea market in **L'Isle-sur-la-Sorgue**, a cool watery town to the east of Avignon (along the N100).

Taking to the water in L'Isle-sur-la-Sorgue

ARLES

4. Roman Morning, Rural Afternoon

A jam-packed morning exploring Arles' Roman, medieval and folkloric legacy followed by lunch at the nearby Bistrot du Paradou. The afternoon is spent buying olive oil from Le Moulin de Jean-Marie Cornille and driving through the rural Alpilles to the Cathédrale d'Images and St-Rémy. Evening spent in Les Baux. 55 km (34 miles).

Arles' Roman arena

The history of **Arles** and much of its character today was shaped by one major factor: it is situated at the head of the Rhône delta on the route linking Italy with Spain. When Rome came into possession of Spain after the defeat of the Carthaginians, Arles became a key strategic town, linking east and west with the valley of the Rhône.

Its vast **Arena** *(amphithéâtre)* is the most potent witness to that time. It is currently undergoing much-needed renovation; those parts that have been restored now give you a good idea of its former grandeur, but it is during a bullfight that the ancient stadium is really brought to life. The bullfight is one of the great events in Arles and a reminder of its long-standing links with Spain.

The other remarkable feature of Arles is the survival of its folk culture, seen in the costumes worn by the Arlesian women during regional festivals. This may lead people to suppose that Arles is the town that is most representative of

Arlesian folk costume

Provence, when, in reality, it is something of a town apart, shaped primarily by its links with Spain and the Camargue.

I like to park on the Boulevard des Lices in the centre of Arles. You will find it by following signs to the Tourist Office. However, if you are coming from north of Arles on the N570 it is better to park near the Place La Martine or along the river. From here it is a 10-minute walk to the centre of town. On market days (Wednesday and Saturday) parking is more difficult.

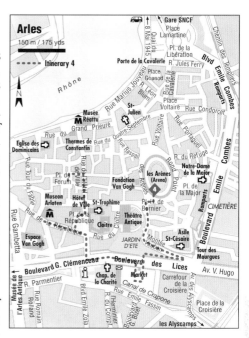

Arles has a good system of *forfaits* (inclusive packages) for visiting the museums and monuments. Though I don't propose you visit all the sites, it is convenient to buy the *Passe Monument*. You can buy this ticket at any monument or at the **Musée de l'Arles Antique** (Avenue de la Première Division Française Libre; open daily; admission fee; tel: 04 90 18 88 88). This is one museum not to be missed, and it is the key to understanding the history of Arles. It is located in a modern building, housing numerous antiquities including statues, carved friezes, pottery, glass, jewellery, mosaics and a collection of marble sarcophagi.

Inside St-Trophime

The **Muséon Arlaten** (29 Rue de la République; open daily July and August, September–June closed Monday; tel: 04 90 93 58 11) is also worth a visit. Founded by the great poet Frédéric Mistral, its theme is that of his life's work, a celebration of the people and the traditional ways of life in the South of France – you will notice that every town in the area has its Rue Frédéric Mistral. As you wander through creaking rooms devoted to furniture, religious legends, *santons*, Provençal customs (for example, the female habit of carrying blessed peach stones to guard against bad luck) costumes, tools and *tableaux* of typical scenes and dramas, you will feel you have stepped back

Bullfighters' bar, Nord-Pinus

in time, a feeling reinforced by the custodians, Arlesian women in traditional dress who sit crocheting in corners.

From the museum walk back to the Place de la République where you will see the church of **St-Trophime**. The tympanum of the Last Judgement in the doorway and the cloisters are masterpieces of medieval architecture. English writer Hilaire Belloc described these cloisters in his book *Hills and the Sea*: 'The cloisters are not only the Middle Ages caught and made eternal, they are also a progression of that great experiment from its youth to its sharp close.'

When you come out again into the sunlight walk around the corner to the **Place du Forum**, where Van Gogh painted *Café de la Nuit*. The Place, with cafés and restaurants and the **Nord-Pinus Hotel** where matadors traditionally reside, at one end, is the focal point of the town's cultural life. The Place has two excellent restaurants; Le Cilantro and the Brasserie de Nord-Pinus *(see pages 74–5)*, but unless you are planning to spend the whole day in Arles you should postpone these pleasures – perhaps make a reservation for the evening – and go instead to the Bistrot du Paradou *(see page 75)* for lunch.

Paradou is a 15-minute drive from Arles. Leave the town on the N570 (direction Avignon) and shortly afterwards turn right onto the D17 for Fontvieille and Paradou. There not a great deal to Paradou other than this one remarkable restaurant, the archetypal working man's café, where lunch is now provided at a (distinctly bourgeois) fixed price of €39, which includes four courses, coffee and the house red wine. At the price I don't believe you can eat a better meal in Provence.

The pleasing village of **Maussane-les-Alpilles** 2km (1 mile) from Paradou is famous for the quality of its olive oil made at **Le Moulin de Jean-Marie Cornille**. The Moulin is only a short way off the main road but the left turn you need to make, though signed, is easy to miss. The mill is a first-class place to buy gifts; in addition to olive oil

Map

les Foutilles · Meynes · Aramon · **Châteaurenard**
St-Gervasy · Comps · Boulbon · Graveson
NÎMES · **Marguerittes** · Vallabrègues
Bodilhan · Manduel · Redessan · Beaucaire · **St-Rémy-de-Provence**
Caissargues · Bouillargues · St-Etienne-du-Grès · Tarascon · les Baux-de-Provence
Garons · Gard · Chaîne des Alpilles · Fontvieille
Bellegarde
Générac · Maussane-les-Alpilles
Église romane · Fourques · **4** · Saint-Martin-de-Crau
St-Gilles · Saliers · **ARLES** · **5**
Franquevaux · Raphèle-les-Arles
Albaron · **PARC NATUREL** · **Bouches-du-Rhône**
le Paty-de-la-Trinité · **de la Camargue** · Plaine de la Crau
Train Touristique · le Sambuc
Étang de Vaccarès
Pioch Badet
Saintes-Maries-de-la-Mer · **DE CAMARGUE** · Peaudure
Golfe des Stes-Maries ou de Beaduc · **Salin-de-Giraud**
Itinerary 4
Itinerary 5
Les Alpilles and the Camargue
10 km / 6.25 miles
Port-St-Louis-du-Rhône

you can buy soaps made with olive oil, *tapenade* (a paste made from black olives) and jams. The four distinctive olive varieties – Saloneque, Béruguette, Verdale and Grossare – create an oil so good that the valley where it is produced (Vallée des Baux) has received its own *appellation d'origine contrôlée*, like a fine wine.

Les Alpilles, a chain of hills 25km (15 miles) long and 6–8km (4–5 miles) wide, rise above this valley, a curious misfit in this otherwise flat area and therefore an ideal site for a stronghold such as Les Baux *(see also page 40)*. From the shady streets of Maussane it is difficult to imagine the existence of this rocky bastion sweltering in the sun only a few kilometres away.

Architectural detail

I would advise against venturing into Les Baux on a hot summer afternoon. You will see the crowds as you approach from Maussane on the D27. It would be far better to pass a cool half an hour in the **Cathédrale d'Images**, then perhaps go down to St-Rémy, returning once more to Les Baux in the early evening.

So, by-passing the village for the time being, make your way to the **Cathédrale d'Images** (Val d'Enfer, Les Baux de Provence; open daily: March–January; admission fee; tel: 04 90 54 38 65), on the D27, one bend above Les Baux. In the giant caverns of white stone left by the extraction of limestone, images are beamed onto the walls and ceilings by 45 slide projectors, accompanied by music. The project has been brilliantly realised and the effects are stunning. The theme changes every year.

If by now it is getting late in the day and you are returning to Arles for the evening, you might want to go straight to Les Baux.

Olive groves in the Vallée des Baux

Otherwise **St-Rémy-de-Provence** is a pleasant 15-minute drive from here (continue on the D27 and at the bottom of the hill turn right onto the D31). It isn't difficult to pass a couple of hours sitting in the bars on the main boulevard or wandering the streets, trying to resist the gorgeous fabrics in Souleiado's window. From here there are two alternatives for returning to Les Baux; either take the D5 past the Roman site of Glanum or, more interestingly, return the way you came taking the D31 and D27. You will pass on the left-hand side one of the workshops where Monsieur Bourges models his *santons*, and as you come over the brow of the hill you have before you the great vista of the Valley of Les Baux with Arles in the far distance.

In the near distance is **Les Baux**. The settlement occupies a prominent place in the mythology of the poetic songsters, the troubadours, and courtly love, which flowered in the courts of the Counts of Provence in the 12th century. The ideal of court life was to live in accordance with a poetic conception of love, which exalted the unsatisfied desire of the lowly knight for the Lady of the Court. A rather frustrating, if romantic, concept.

The ruins of the castle built by the Lords of Les Baux, where this concept was enacted, occupy the highest point of the site. You will not be disappointed if you make the effort to climb to the highest point of these ruins. Below is the village of Les Baux, a mixture of restored Renaissance houses and ruins. Abandoned in the 17th century, this is now one of the most-visited ancient sites in France. The entrance is via the Musée d'Histoire des Baux/Citadel (Rue de Trencart; open daily; admission fee; tel: 04 90 54 55 56).

To return to Arles, follow the signs to Fontvieille (D17) and turn left when you reach the junction with the N570. An evening in Arles is best spent at one of the restaurants in the Place du Forum, but if you are lucky there may be an event at the **Arena** or at the **Théâtre Antique**.

Les Baux's castle blends into the cliffs

The best way of seeing the Camargue

5. The Camargue

If you leave Arles on the D570 going south, you quickly enter a landscape of lagoons, rice fields and salt marshes, populated by cowboys, bulls and flamingos. This area, contained within the two arms of the Rhône river, is called the Camargue.

The Camargue is an entity the French would call *très spéciale*. Though part of the *département* of the Bouches-du-Rhône and belonging to the *commune* (district) of Arles, it is a place apart, probably having more rapport with France to the west than the east.

There are really two separate Camargues. One is covered with rice fields, salt pans, stud farms and cattle ranches, and cannot easily be visited. The other is the nature reserve of the **Etang de Vaccarès**. Though containing an extraordinary diversity of wildlife, it is known above all for the flamingos (estimated at 50,000) that rest here in the spring and summer. Contact the tourist office in either Arles or Saintes-Marie-de-la-Mer *(see page 91)* for hiking maps and information on visiting the area on horseback or by boat.

The main town of the Camargue is **Saintes-Maries-de-la-Mer**, enshrined in Provençal legend as the landing point of the Boat of Bethany which brought Mary Jacobé (the sister of the Virgin), Mary Salomé, Mary Magdalene and, as one history of Provence has aptly put it, 'half the cast of the New Testament'.

Saintes-Maries-de-la-Mer is an enjoyable town to visit, above all because of the vast beaches – in the summer you should allow at least an hour to travel the 38km (23.5 miles) from Arles. Access to the nature reserve is from the D36.

Be aware that the Camargue has very little tourist infrastructure because living here is almost impossible. The only people who tolerate the conditions are the cowboys, who rear the bulls, and environmentalists. The main plague is the mosquitoes, particularly from March to October. As a protected environment the Camargue has never been de-mosquitoed, so take cream with you. The best time to visit is probably when the mistral *(see page 82)* is scattering the insects.

Aix-en-Provence

6. From the Renaissance to Cézanne

A morning tour of the elegant Renaissance town of Aix and an afternoon exploring Cézanne country.

The first Roman settlement in Provence was founded by the proconsul Sextius Calvinus after his victory over the Franks. He named it Aquae Sextiae, alluding equally to its founder and the thermal springs near the settlement. It became one of the most important Roman towns in Provence and a major halt on the Aurelian Way, the road connecting the Italian border with the valley of the Rhône. This

Door decoration in Aix

is the site of **Aix-en-Provence** today. Virtually nothing survives in modern-day Aix from this period of its history. However, the position of Aix on one of the main routes connecting Paris with Nice is a reminder that the main roads of Provence follow the paths of their Roman counterparts.

From the 12th century, when the Counts of Provence had their court at Aix, it developed as a centre of learning and the arts. The university was founded in 1409 by Louis II of Anjou. His second son René, who became Duke of Anjou, Count of Provence (known in Provençal folklore as Good King René), was an enlightened patron of the arts. He made Aix the focal point for artists in Provence, as Avignon had been a century earlier under the popes.

The university and patronage of the arts do more than anything to shape the life of Aix today. The town is full of students and the annual festival of music is said to rival those of Bayreuth and Salzburg (doubtful).

It is relatively easy to find your way in and out

Breakfast at Deux Garçons

of Aix by car. When you reach the ring road follow the signs for the *Office du Tourisme* at Place du Général de Gaulle. The main car parks are located here, close to the fountain marking the western end of **Cours Mirabeau**, which is named in honour of the famous Count of Mirabeau of 1789 who was the representative of Aix in Paris. This shaded avenue, with its four fountains and elegant buildings, every other one either a café or a

One of the fountains of Aix

bookshop, is the heart of Aix today. It is a potent symbol of the sophisticated and cultured lifestyle of its inhabitants.

Days in Aix should always begin here, preferably drinking coffee in **Le Café des Deux Garçons** (53*bis* Cours Mirabeau). Long-time meeting-place of writers and intellectuals, its interior is classic 19th-century *brasserie* style, with wooden chairs, marble-topped tables, gilt mirrors and brass lamps.

The Cours Mirabeau was built in the second half of the 17th century as a *cours à carrosses,* a street for horse-drawn carriages,

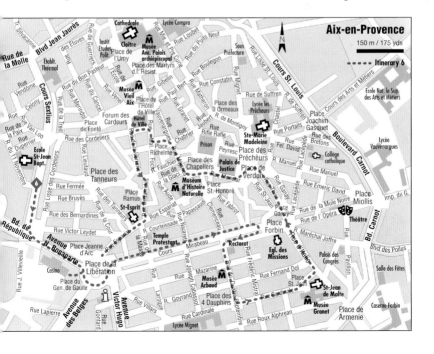

a symbol of the increasing prosperity of Aix, capital town of Provence and seat of the court of justice. The area to the south of the Cours, known as the **Quartier Mazarin**, was developed during the 18th century, on the model of an Italian Renaissance town. Fronted by the grand mansions *(les hôtels particuliers)* on the Cours, the area rapidly became a fashionable address for the wealthy, who had previously lived in the old town.

One of the finest of the grand mansions in this area is No. 38, Hôtel Maurel de Pontevès. Its facade superimposes the three classical decorative orders – Doric, Ionic and Corinthian – and is notable for the

The decorative Hôtel de Ville

sculptured figures supporting the balcony above the doorway. The figures represent Atlantis, who in Greek mythology bore the weight of the world on his shoulders. As you walk around the town you will probably notice this classical motif duplicated on numerous smaller balconies.

In the middle of the Cours is a moss-encrusted fountain. Fed by a thermal spring, it was originally called the Fontaine Chaude (hot), but is now more often referred to as the mossy fountain, Fontaine Moussue. From here walk down the Rue du 4 Septembre into the Quartier Mazarin. You quickly reach **La Place des Quatre Dauphins**, ornamented by a superb baroque fountain. This is the finest of all the ornamental fountains which adorn Aix.

Walking west from the Place along the Rue Cardinale you come to the **Museé Granet** (Place St-Jean-de-Malte; closed Tuesday; admission fee; tel: 04 42 38 14 70), the most interesting museum in Aix (closed for renovation until June 2006). It houses a fine collection of paintings, including a dozen or so by Cézanne, illustrating the main themes of his work.

Located at the top of Rue Cardinale is Rue d'Italie, where you

A long tradition of sweet-making

will find the Confiserie Brémond Fils, one of the oldest firms making the famous *calissons* of Aix: a boat-shaped confectionery of sweet almond paste blended with crystallised oranges and melons softened in fruit syrup (often apricot). In popular folklore these sweets have attained the status of a kind of Host and are dispensed in church at Christmas, Easter and on 1 September, to mark the end of the great plague of 1630.

Crossing Place Forbin, you leave the Mazarin Quarter and enter the old town. This maze of streets north of the Cours Mirabeau is a shoppers' paradise. In the morning the market on the Place Richelme is a colourful sight. Later in the day this is the place to come for bars and it is a relaxed alternative to the Cours. Behind the Post Office – an elegant 18th-century building that once housed the corn market – is the **Hôtel de Ville**. Built in the 17th century, it shows all the decorative motifs of the baroque style: pediments, friezes and the curling forms of flowers and fruit. Inside, the courtyard has a lovely harmony of forms and superb examples of that particularly French urban craft, *ferronnerie d'art* (art metalwork). To the north is **Cathédrale St-Sauveur** with its cloister and Nicolas Froment's 15th-century triptych *Mary in the Burning Bush*. Next door, the Baroque **Palais de l'Archevêché** contains a **Musée des Tapisseries** (Tapestry Museum; closed Tuesday; admission fee; tel: 04 42 23 09 91).

Towards midday in summer the temperature in Aix can climb high and the light becomes very clear – a phenomenon described by Charles Dickens: 'The town was... so hot, and so intensely light, that when I walked out at noon it was like coming suddenly from the darkened room into crisp blue fire. The air was so very clear, that distant hills and rocky points appeared within an hour's walk...'

It may be that Dickens was referring to the distant outline of the **Mont Ste-Victoire**. It is less than an hour's walk from the centre of Aix to the foothills of this mountain (15 minutes by car). Note

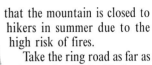

that the mountain is closed to hikers in summer due to the high risk of fires.

Take the ring road as far as the turning for **Le Tholonet**, the D17, known as *'route Cézanne'*. Within minutes the boundaries of Aix are left behind and each bend in the road offers a glimpse of the mountain. When you reach Le Tholonet, you will see on your left a château (the headquarters of La Société du Canal de Provence). On your right is an avenue of plane trees leading to a park.

Cézanne never tired of painting this area dominated by the Mont Ste-Victoire. He wrote to his son: 'I spend every day in this landscape with its beautiful shapes. Indeed I cannot imagine a more pleasant way or place to pass my time.' Le Tholonet presents a number of different options for passing the afternoon. Either you can adjourn to the park, a favourite promenade for the Auxois, or you can take one of a number of walks from various car parks along the D17 between Le Tholonet and Puyloubier. The landscape is fierce and hot in summer, recognisably the one Cézanne shaped on his canvases. Alternatively, you can make a complete circuit (74km/46 miles) of the mountain, via Puyloubier, Pourrières, the D23 (direction Rians), branching left onto the D223 (D10; direction Vauvenargues) and from there back to Aix along the D10. The journey will take you through spectacular rocky landscapes, the vineyards of the Côte de Provence estates and give you a view of the north face of the mountain. This area so captivated Pablo Picasso that he bought the château

Picasso's château at Vauvenargues

in Vauvenargues (unfortunately this site is not open to the public). For a complete circuit bringing you back to the Cours Mirabeau you should allow around two hours.

You should be back in Aix in time for an apéritif and the *promenade* on the Cours, and perhaps supper at the **2G** (the familiar name for the Café des Deux Garçons), where you breakfasted.

Basilica of St Victor, Marseille

7. Marseille

Marseille, France's second city after Paris, is less than 30 minutes' drive from Aix-en-Provence (by way of the A51 motorway). It can be seedy, as every port city, though it is currently undergoing something of a renaissance. The contrasts with the sedate splendour of Aix are marked, though the inhabitants of Marseille are supremely laid-back.

The appeal of Marseille is unconventional. If you are going to pay a short evening or morning visit, here are a few reference points. The restaurants of the Vieux Port are famous for *bouillabaisse*; Miramar, in particular, is an institution *(see page 75)*. Place Thiars, just off the southeast corner of the port, has restaurants and clubs open all night. The other main night spot, trendier than the port, is the **Cours Julien**, a 15-minute walk from the old port up La Canebière (Marseille's swanky shopping boulevard).

The best strategy for a short visit is to explore the area of the Vieux Port, and then climb up to the Cathedral of Notre Dame de la Garde, perched on a hill that dominates the city. The view is splendid. Alternatively, go out to the Palais du Pharo, on the spur of the port, for another great view over the city. From here drive along the Corniche Président J. F. Kennedy to the Vallon des Auffes, an old Mediterranean fishing port, where you will find several good fish restaurants.

On the quay

ALONG THE COAST

In 1887 the French writer Stephen Liégeard, inspired by the deep blue of the southern French coast, came up with the enduring headline, *La Côte d'Azur* (Azure Coast). Though this describes the whole coastal area equally well, the coast within the compass of this guide – from Marseille to St-Tropez – is more generally known as *La Côte Provençale*. If you want to go further east along the coast to Cannes and Nice, I recommend you buy a copy of either *Insight Guide: French Riviera* or the *Insight Pocket Guide: French Riviera*.

The three itineraries that follow have selected highlights from the Côte Provençale and each could easily make a day. The overall scheme is linear, linking Cassis and St-Tropez, two towns connected by 100km (60 miles) of twisting coastal roads; a magnificent drive on a crisp winter's day, a crawling caravan of traffic in summer.

By the end of the year 2004 it was calculated that of the 34 million visitors to Provence and the Riviera, two-thirds came to the coast and the majority of those in the summer months. A quick, impressionistic tour of the coast can, of course, be made in the high season, but I fear the impression would not be a good one. My advice, if you only have one day in the summer, is to enjoy one good itinerary. And always have a swimming costume at the ready.

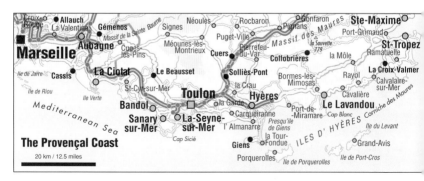

The Provençal Coast

20 km / 12.5 miles

Boats of all sizes along the Côte Provençale

8. Cassis

This itinerary consists of a trip to the busy old port of Cassis, messing about in boats in the beautiful 'calanques', a fish lunch in one of numerous great-value restaurants down by the port and some shopping for fine wines.

Cassis is 30 minutes by motorway from Aix-en-Provence; leave Aix on the A8 (direction Fréjus/Nice), turn south onto the A52 (direction Aubagne and then Toulon), take the last exit for Cassis, entering the town on the D559. Parking is never easy but early in the morning you should find a space in the car park next to the port.

The three things I believe should shape any visit to Cassis are: a swim in the wonderful waters of the fjord-like *calanques (see next page)*, a fish lunch in the port and a taste of the aromatic white wines produced in the surrounding hillsides.

The port of Cassis has a feeling of expectancy in the morning. Fishermen are landing the catch from the previous night under the careful eye of the restaurant proprietors and the boats that ply up and down the coast are waiting to begin their daily shuttles. You can pick up a list of the trips on offer from a hut on the quay and then plan your morning over a coffee in one of the port's many bars.

Between Cassis and Marseille the coastline is a massive series

Fish on the move in Cassis

'Calanque' boat trip

of limestone cliffs, rising as high as 400m (1,300ft), indented with long, narrow channels of water – known as *calanques.* They were formed when the sea invaded the narrow river valleys between these cliffs at the end of the Ice Age. Some of them end in a small beach, others are hemmed in by white walls of rock that rise sheer from the water. The water has both a translucence and a density of colour that is astonishing. The cost of visiting the *calanques* depends both on which ones you choose and for how long you go. The nearest ones to Cassis are Port-Miou, Port Pin and En Vau. Make sure that you take a boat that stops for swimming.

The *calanques* can also be visited on foot. The Tourist Office will sell you a map of the *randonnées* (hikes) in the area, though you will probably find the paths are closed in summer due to the ever-present fire risk.

'La route des Crêtes' to Bandol

Aim to return from the *calanques* in time for a fish lunch in the port. The **Quai des Baux** has a great line of venues, notably L'Oustau de la Mar, Bar le Port, Chez César and Chez Gilbert.

If you are staying in Cassis and would like an afternoon excursion or you are moving down the coast in the direction of Bandol, you should take *la route des Crêtes*, the D141 to La Ciotat, along the magnificent cliffs of **Cap Canaille**. This road also has the advantage of passing the **Clos Ste-Magdeleine**, where one of the finest white wines of Cassis is produced. The road twists for 13km (8 miles) up to the **Sémaphore du Bec de l'Aigle** – Eagle's Beak Point – for a vertiginous view over the whole of this unique coastline.

From Eagle's Beak Point continue to La Ciotat and follow the D40 until it links up with the D559 to Bandol. The town of **Bandol**, a seemingly endless seafront of bright boutiques and crowded beaches, you can safely bypass; the wines of Bandol you cannot. The town gives its name to one of the really great red wines of Provence and to one of the finest rosé wines in the world. The rosé somehow manages to be both light and full-bodied, the best of all drinks on a hot summer day. It can be hard to find as the best

producers jealously guard their Mourvèdre grapes to produce the rich red wines with their complex bouquets of fruit and herbs.

Many of the producers are located near the medieval villages of **La Cadière d'Azur** and **Le Castellet**; you will see signs for them before Bandol. They are more marked by the demands of tourism than the perched villages in the Vaucluse, but camped high in the hills they have the usual commanding views.

My favourite Bandol producer is **Domaine Tempier** (just off the D82 north of the city map), where you are guaranteed a warm welcome from the Peyraud family and a good *dégustation*.

9. Ile de Porquerolles

The Ile de Porquerolles is the largest of the three **Iles d'Hyères**. These islands are an image of an older Mediterranean coast – a coast that was sparsely populated and densely forested, with beaches that are just a dash of sand separating trees and water. The easiest and cheapest way to reach Porquerolles is by ferry from the **Presqu'île de Giens**, near Hyères. If you are coming from the direction of Bandol there is no need to go into Hyères. After the port of Toulon, take the D559 to Carqueiranne and cross to the Presqu'île on the isthmus behind the Plage de l'Almanarre. Windsurfers note: this beach has the best conditions in the south of France.

The ferries leave from **La Tour Fondue** daily to serve the island's permanent population of 300 people. In July and August they run every thirty minutes between 8.30am and 7.30pm; at other times check the timetables (tel: 04 94 58 21 81). The service takes approximately 20 minutes and the round trip costs €15.

The island is 7km (4 miles) long and 3km (2 miles) wide, well within the scope of walkers. The ideal mode of transport is the mountain bike (don't bother taking a touring bike on the ferry, as the paths are too rough for them). They can be hired from the village of Porquerolles (about €12 a day), though demand exceeds supply in the summer. Before I leave you to enjoy this lovely island here are a few tips: pick up a map of the island from the Tourist Office in Hyères or the information booth in the village and collect provisions before leaving the village; there is no water on the island and no beach cafés once you leave the vicinity of the port.

Finally, ensure you have enough time to get back for the last ferry.

A sailboarder's mecca

St-Tropez – the Vieux Port, the village, the Citadel; Pampelonne and its famous beaches; the hill towns of Gassin and Ramatuelle; the wines of Château Minuty; the Place des Lices and the Café des Arts.

A brief history: from time immemorial St-Tropez has been a village of the sea, home of fishermen, mariners and privateers. The port is an excellent mooring. In 1892 Paul Signac, the pontillist painter, came to St-Tropez and stayed, bewitched by the light, the deserted beaches and the little village of fishermen. The writer Colette lived here in the 1920s, already complaining of the crowds. During World War II, on 15 August 1944, the port was mined and destroyed; 3,000 parachutists descended on the town, while the Americans landed on the beach of Pampelonne.

The 1960s heralded Brigitte Bardot and the filming of *And God Created Woman*. St-Tropez became known internationally and its demise was forecast regularly during the 1960s, 70s and 80s. But today it is enduringly popular. Why? I think because it manages to be both a Provençal fishing village and port, and the very image of the *dolce vita*. The Place des Lices is the rendezvous for the local *boulistes* and where the celebrities come for an *apéritif*. The Baie de Pampelonne is filled with expensive boats and beautiful people; the sandy beach 5km (3 miles) long, is backed not by a concrete jungle but by farms and vineyards. Then there is the port and the nightlife. In this setting everyone has a chance to live out their

Beach bar, St-Tropez

dreams. I consider St-Tropez to be one of France's great places, but in summer it needs to be approached with care.

If you are just coming here for one day, try to arrive before 9am and leave after 10pm – a good day in St-Tropez is a long one. The N98 into St-Tropez divides into a one-way system as you reach the town; follow this until you reach Place Blanqui where you will see signs for the large Parking du Port. It is rarely a good idea to take your car further than this. You can get a good map from the Tourist Office on the Quai Jean Jaurès in the old port.

The morning is the time to wander past the boats that embellish the *quai* and to drink a *café glacé* in one of the famous bars, such

52

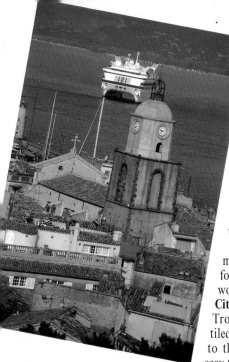

View from the Citadel

as **Sénéquier** or **Le Gorille**. Never seeming to move, these boats are an essential part of the show. From the *quai*, walk into the heart of the old village via Place de la Mairie. The village is a nocturnal creature in summer and you will find the shops gingerly opening their doors only at 10am.

Around 11 o'clock you might be thinking of leaving for the beaches, but first it is worth walking up to the **Citadel**, the old fort above St-Tropez. As you look over the tiled roofs and the clock tower to the Gulf of St-Tropez, it is easy to understand why the town has become such an icon of the South of France. Try and visit the Musée de l'Annonciade near the old port, with its excellent collection of modern masters, many of whom painted in St-Tropez (July–mid-October open daily; rest of year closed Tuesday; admission fee; tel: 04 94 17 84 10).

St-Tropez has two beaches within walking distance, the Plage des Graniers and the Plage de la Bouillabaisse, but for the real glamour factor, you must drive round to the **Plage de Pampelonne**

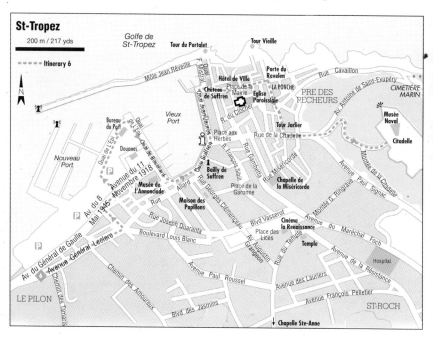

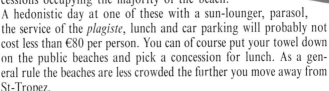

Tahiti-Plage

(from the car park head out of the town and after about 1km/ ⅝ mile) turn right onto the D93 *route des Plages*). As you drive along the *route des Plages* you will see signs for **Tahiti-Plage**, **Bora-Bora**, **Club 55**, **Nioulargo**, some of the famous concessions occupying the majority of the beach.

A hedonistic day at one of these with a sun-lounger, parasol, the service of the *plagiste*, lunch and car parking will probably not cost less than €80 per person. You can of course put your towel down on the public beaches and pick a concession for lunch. As a general rule the beaches are less crowded the further you move away from St-Tropez.

If by 5pm you find the charms of the beach are palling, or the heat is overbearing, the late afternoon sea breezes will be cooling **Ramatuelle** and **Gassin**, two hill towns situated behind Pampelonne. Gassin, perhaps the finer of the two, though less of a living village than Ramatuelle, has the advantage of being home to **Château Minuty** (on the D61 between Gassin and St-Tropez), an estate producing some of the finest wines in the Côte de Provence. The white and rosé wines designated *cuveé de l'Oratoire* are exceptional.

If at all possible, I'd recommend avoiding St-Tropez between the hours of 5pm and 8pm, when it is far more pleasant to be walking in the vineyards of Château Minuty. For me this is the low point of St-Tropez's day – hot and crowded. One fine option is to have an early supper in the cool perfection of Gassin. However, you must be back in time to witness an important part of the St-Tropez experience: the evening promenade in the **Place des Lices** with an apéritif or a coffee in the **Café des Arts**.

Place des Lices by night

11. A Circuit in the Hills

A day's ride through forests of pine and oak, vineyards and olive trees; stopping to see the Château of Entrecasteaux; swim in a waterfall and visit the market town of Aups. 60km (37 miles).

This part of the Var, whilst recognisably a part of the Provence you have been travelling through, is in many ways different. The first thing you will notice as you cross the A8 *autoroute du soleil* (the great divide in Provence) is the change in the pace of life; it is slow. This is a rural area but it is without the great agricultural riches of the alluvial plains which surround the Rhône. The forests of pine and oak are broken by vineyards and olive trees but not by endless fields of melons. As a result the culinary tradition is poorer, with much reliance on *soupe au pistou* and *aïoli (see pages 70–1)*, and the superb menu for just €15 becomes increasingly difficult to find.

Similarly the wine is much poorer than closer to the Rhône; each village has a co-operative, but the wines are not of a high quality. Domaine St-Jean and Château Thuerry in Villecroze, producing good, sometimes excellent, red and rosé wines, are the only estates worth a special visit.

The villages are simpler than those in the Bouches-de-Rhône, the masons not having around them the tremendous forms of the Romans, who merely passed by this area as they hurried along the Aurelian Way from Fréjus to Aix. But they have their own charm, their *cours*, cafés and *boulistes* and their superb *campaniles* – the structures of ornamental metalwork that adorn the ubiquitous bell towers and cage the bells.

Climbing up into the Var

Salernes is a good starting point. From the direction of St-Tropez it is a 30-minute drive from Le Muy (at the junction of the

Window in Salernes

D25 and the A8/N7) via the N555 to Draguignan and the D557 then turn left on D560. At first sight there is nothing remarkable about Salernes; it only really gets going when the *cours* is filled by the market on Wednesday and Sunday. However, it is identified in France (and world-wide) with the superb work of its *céramistes*. At one time as many as 50 factories were producing *tomettes*, the small red hexagonal tiles that cover the floors in nearly all the older houses in Provence. Today the local clays are not only turned into *terre cuite* for floors; the glazes and designs of the ceramicists transform the humble clay into superb decorative objects – tiles for kitchens and bathrooms, lamps and bowls. You will see the showrooms as you approach Salernes on the D560; they are interesting to visit and great for presents.

From Salernes it is 8km (5 miles) to **Entrecasteaux** along the D31, which follows the winding course of the River Bresque. Just out of Salernes on the right-hand side is a series of pillars clothed in mauve tiling marking the showroom of Alain Vagh, one of the 20 ceramic manufacturers in Salernes. His passion is to tile everything in sight, including cars and cement mixers. His beautiful tiles and ceramics are also on sale in Villecroze and Ramatuelle.

As you turn the corner by the football pitch the massive **Château d'Entrecasteaux** (April–September guided tours daily; October–March groups only by appointment; admission fee; tel: 040 94 04 43 95) comes into view, bearing down on the small village of the

same name. It was originally an 11th-century fortress, but the classically simple facade you see today dates from the 17th and 18th centuries, when it hosted among others the diarist Madame de Sévigné. One of the most interesting parts of its history is that you wouldn't see it at all today if it had not been rescued from ruin in 1974 by Scottish painter, adventurer and soldier Ian McGarvie-Munn. The château has recently been entirely refurbished with period furniture, tapestries and works of art, and is now inhabited by its new owner, Alain Gayral. You can contemplate the vagaries of history and drink a beer in one of the bars opposite the château, before lunching in Cotignac.

The road to Cotignac (D50) comes up as a sharp right turn shortly after you leave Entrecasteaux. It winds for 8km (5 miles) through vineyards that just sneak into the Côtes de Provence appellation. You will see the big wine co-operative as you come into **Cotignac**. Turn left at this point, drive towards the main *cours* and leave the car in the car park on the left. From here you will enter the village at the bottom of its magnificent central *cours*, one of the finest in the Var, shaded by beautiful old plane trees and surrounded by houses dating from the 16th, 17th and 18th centuries. Before settling down to lunch it is also well worth walking up to the Place de la Mairie to take a look at the marvellous *campanile*.

The small market town of **Aups**, situated at the foot of the mountain of the Espiguières (one of the first spurs of the Alps), is your next destination. The D22 from Cotignac to Aups passes through **Sillans-la-Cascade** where, just under a kilometre (⅝ mile) from the village, the River Bresque falls 42m (138ft) over a cliff into a deep pool. This is a well-known beauty spot and it is usually pretty crowded during the summer months; however, the walk is enjoyable, and the water is cold, making it a good place for

Alain Vagh has tiled his jeep

a refreshing swim. The path to the waterfall leaves the village from the corner of the road just under the castle tower.

Aups, as befits the chief town of the area, is a bustling place. In summer it is one of the few towns filled with visitors. The town is

crowned by a fine 16th-century clock-tower adorned with a sundial. Aups has a strong tradition of republican resistance and it was the scene of many popular uprisings in the 19th century.

In the winter it puts on another hat, and devotes itself to *la chasse* (the hunt); every restaurant has wild boar pâté and rabbit stew on its menu and the streets are empty. You should enjoy walking around Aups; the air is very pure and the light has excellent luminosity. On Thursday mornings between November and February, Aups hosts one of the largest truffle markets in all of France. Prices are steep – as much as €600 per kilo – for this fragrant fungus, and transactions are discreetly concluded in muffled whispers.

When you leave Aups, no matter where you are staying, you should drive the 10km (6 miles) along the D77 to **Tourtour**. The name of this village of breathtaking views and medieval vaulted passageways is said to derive from the Celtic word 'tur', meaning highest point, and if you go up to the highest point by L'Eglise St-Denis (towards sunset is the perfect time or when the mistral is sweeping the skies clear), you will be rewarded with a stunning sight. The village has built a very fine observation point locating surrounding landmarks. The *place du village*, with the fountain in the middle, is a tempting place to have a drink and a meal. But if the day has not rolled on too quickly the last stop of the day is only a hairpin bend or two away on the D51.

Villecroze-les-Grottes has none of the obvious glories of Tourtour, though the park and the old village are certainly worth visiting: note the massive walls of the château and the fountain in the wall in Rue de France. Above all in Villecroze you get the feeling that life being lived to the full. The bars are busy and the *boulistes* are invariably playing in the finely proportioned *cours*, bounded on one side by the village school. If you time your visit right, the music academy will be hosting a concert or the town's rugby team will be playing a match in Villecroze. If none of these things is happening, however, don't despair – **La Cascade** is a good spot for a drink and a meal.

Villecroze-les-Grottes

A 99-km (60-mile), three-hour circuit that leaves from Aups and takes in the Lac de Ste-Croix and the breathtakingly beautiful Grand Canyon du Verdon, one of Provence's most notable natural wonders.

Aups is frequently referred to as the 'gateway to the Alps', because the D957 leaving the town to the north climbs very rapidly into high mountain country. Within the space of around 30 minutes, you should reach the limits of the Var, and if you drive across the Pont du Galetas at the bottom of the Grand Canyon du Verdon you will make your first entrance into the *département* of Alpes de Haute-Provence.

The Grand Canyon du Verdon is one of the great natural sights in Europe, a savage slash in the earth, measuring 21km (13 miles) long and at times no more than 6m (18ft) wide, compressed between vertiginous rock faces rising as high as 700m (2,296ft).

The instrument of this work is the River Verdon, now regulated by dams at Chaudanne and Castellane and flowing peacefully into the **Lac de Ste-Croix**.

A complete circuit of the canyon by car will normally take around three hours, depending on how many of the excellent photographic opportunities you manage to resist. It is rumoured that in August the volume of traffic can stretch this to 5 hours. If you are coming from Aups, the best point of attack is probably Aiguines. From here follow the D71, known as the *corniche sublime*. Constructed in 1925 to serve the new obsession with touring by motor car, the *corniche* is designed to take in the full effect of the canyon. It succeeds magnificently.

The Grand Canyon du Verdon

From the D71 take the D90 to Trigance and then the D955 north until the junction with the D952, the old Castellane road. At St-Clair, 33km (20 miles) later, turn left onto the D957 returning to Aups.

The Luberon

13. Le Pays d'Apt

Perched villages – Roussillon, Gordes, Bonnieux; Cistercian simplicity and splendour; glacé fruits and the fruity wines of the Côtes du Luberon. Approximately 70km (45 miles).

From a base in Apt the day is a roller-coaster ride through a small area bounded on one side by the Plateau de Vaucluse and on the other by the mountains of the Luberon. This area is generally known as the Luberon, though locally it is more often referred to as Le Pays d'Apt.

Apt was a considerable Roman colony, situated on the route of the Domitian Way, the great road connecting the Alpine towns of Sisteron and Briançon to the northeast with the Rhône valley. Just 16km (10 miles) west of Apt, where the Domitian Way crossed the River Calavon, you can see the Pont Julien, one of the best-preserved Roman bridges in France. As you travel through this region you will be constantly reminded of past cultures.

The Luberon also has great agricultural riches. Partially screened from the mistral by the hills of the Vaucluse, it has the ideal climate for fruit growing and has made Cavaillon (on the western edge of the Luberon) into France's great fruit market. If you enter the Pays d'Apt from the *arrière pays* (back country) of the Var you will see the transition from endless forest to line after line of fruit trees.

Market in Apt

Mural in Roussillon

The town of Apt is in permanent anticipation of Saturday, when the centre of gravity of the Luberon tilts east and the streets are filled with a maelstrom of marketeers. You will not find much to detain you on other days but it is a good base from which to explore the Luberon, as you can generally find a hotel room without booking months in advance. A coffee in the **Brasserie Grégoire**, opposite the Tourist Office on Place de la Bouquerie, will set you up for the day.

Apt is famous for its glacé fruits in the way that Aix is famous for its *calissons* – both make good presents. You will pass the **Kerry Aptunion** factory on your way to Roussillon about 3km (2 miles) outside Apt on the N100. It has a retail outlet selling the many varieties of glacé fruits as well as other classic Provençal products. Shortly after the factory, you will see the first signs for **Roussillon**. The most spectacular approach is from the D227 (the third turning to Roussillon off the D4 from the direction of Apt), the village coming into view on a precipitous cliff that has lent its many hues of red to the *crépi* (cement rendering) of the houses.

The position of Roussillon is probably more spectacular now than when it was built, for two centuries of erosion and commercial exploitation of the ochre deposits have left it surrounded by red and gold rock formations, gullies and cliffs. They can be

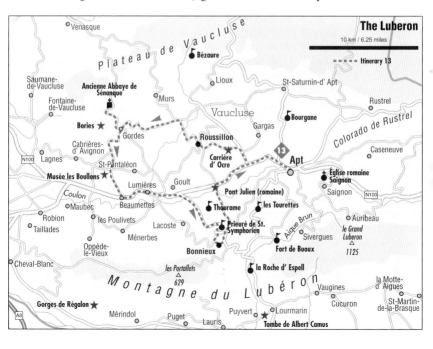

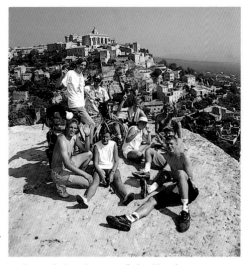

explored by a footpath that leaves from behind the car park on the east side of the village, though they are best avoided if it is very hot or wet. You should not, however, miss the outstanding panorama over the Ventoux and the Luberon from the *plateforme du rocher* at the top of the village. To the northwest you can see the town of **Gordes**, built on a promontory of rock at the foot of the plateau of the Vaucluse.

Gordes is dominated by its castle and church, best seen from the approach road (D15); however, before entering the town you might like to visit the **Village des Bories**, which you will see signposted from the road.

Bories are dry stone huts made of concentric layers of flat, unmortared slabs of limestone. Seemingly primitive, they are in fact quite complex and difficult to reproduce. No one knows when they were first built, or by whom, but some have been dated back to the Bronze Age. over the centuries, *bories* served many functions, from shepherd's shelters, to bread ovens, to cramped quarters on the family farm. It is estimated that there are as many as 3,000 of them in Provence, most of them isolated but occasionally found in groups, such as this one near Gordes. The *bories* are now home to a museum of rural life (daily 9am–sunset; admission fee, tel: 04 90 72 03 48).

Dry-stone borie

As recently as the 18th century these hardy constructions were still being built, using the same techniques and materials as the Celtic-Ligurian tribes used some 3,000 years ago.

You can park in the middle of Gordes and, although it is crowded in the summer, this is probably a better bet than a hot walk up the hill. If you have visited the *bories* you will be in need, almost certainly, of a drink or two. The **Café de la Renaissance** in the small square behind the castle is likely to be welcome. Here, in the shadow of the walls, you can weigh the pros and cons of visiting the castle. The pros: the entrance is right in front of you, the castle contains a fine Renaissance fireplace and the views from the battlements are superb. The cons: the castle was extensively damaged during World War II, then scrupulously restored from ruin by the Op-art artist Victor Vasarely and now exhibits modern art. If you come out in favour of eating, an excellent meal can be had at Le Bouquet de Basilic nearby on Routes de Murs *(see page 77)*.

Before you leave Gordes in the afternoon it is worth casting an eye over the **church of St-Firmin**. Built in the 18th century, it is remarkable for having retained its original polychrome decoration.

In the 12th century France saw the founding of the second great monastic order, the Cistercian, by monks anxious to return to the original strictness of the Benedictine rule. Their leader, St-Bernard, espoused solitude and silence and favoured architecture of simple, harmonious forms to facilitate contemplation. They began to build abbeys which would conform to these ideals and one of them was in the isolated Sénancole valley near Gordes.

The abbey of **Sénanque** (4km/2 miles from Gordes on the D177) in the Sénancole valley is a sight for sore eyes. When you look at it from the east over the lavender fields, which are in bloom in late June to early July, it has a perfection of form that is unforgettable. Even if you go no further than this point the journey will have been worthwhile.

The monks have recently returned and the abbey can be visited (guided visits only, call ahead for hours; tel: 04 90 72 05 72). The building you see on the right-hand side of the valley is the refectory, with an exhibition devoted to the life of the Cistercian order.

It is now time to travel to the **perched villages** on the opposite side of the valley: Oppède, Ménerbes, Lacoste, Bonnieux, whose names make up the modern litany of the Luberon. They have – along with the other villages of the Luberon – a turbulent history. Many were partly destroyed in the religious conflicts of the 16th century, but Bonnieux enjoyed great prosperity as a papal fiefdom until the Revolution. By the 1950s they were falling into ruin, ravaged by time and rural depopulation. At this point they were 'rediscovered' by artists and writers looking for an idyllic rural habitat, and the process of restoration began. Today there is hardly a house left to be restored and, though visitors course through the narrow streets, the villages have certainly not lost their appeal.

All of the above villages can be recommended for one reason or another but I have picked out **Bonnieux**, for the fine views across the valley over to Lacoste, the steep streets bordered by grand *hôtels particuliers*, the bakery museum and an excellent producer of Côtes du Luberon wine.

From Gordes, Bonnieux is around 21km (13 miles) away. To get there, take the D2 (direction Cavaillon), turn left onto the D103

St-Firmin

(direction Beaumettes), turn left onto the N100 and then right to Bonnieux on the D36.

It's not always easy to find parking in Bonnieux, but the nearer you manage to park to the Hôtel César *(see page 88)* – on the right as you come through the village – the less you will have to climb. Opposite the César a cobbled street runs to the top of the village. Continue up Rue de la République and you will arrive first at Rue de la Mairie, leading to the *belvédère* and a lovely panorama out over the Luberon countryside.

Located further up Rue de la République, at No. 12, is the **Musée de la Boulangerie** (Bakery Museum; open April–October, closed Tuesday; admission fee; tel: 04 90 75 88 34). The museum has been well put together, although it is disappointing in some details: I would have liked more information on types of bread and the skills of the *boulanger*.

My favourite place in Bonnieux is the **Château la Canorgue** and its fine wines. The château is located a little way past the wide corner at the bottom of the village, along the D149 (direction Pont Julien). The château is archetypal Provence, fading yellow in a shady courtyard with an overgrown ornamental basin in the garden below. The wines produced are atypical of the region, in that red, white and róse are all good. The delicious white wine has a surprising length of fruit and the reds keep extremely well.

With a few bottles of wine in the boot of your car, you might like to finish the day by staying on the D149 to the **Pont Julien** and then, if the time is right, go back to the D4 and find a point where you can watch the setting sun turn the gorgeous ochre hues of Roussillon to gold.

Château la Canorgue

Shopping

Shopping in Provence is one of the best ways of meeting the people who live here. I say meeting them because Provence is not the sort of place where you 'grab and buy'. Shopping is often a slow process; whether you are a profitable visitor or a regular customer, the social aspect of buying takes precedence over the commercial. In the *boucherie* (butcher's), for example, the prolonged discussion of the relative merits of this week's *gigot* (lamb roast), is considered more crucial than serving the long queue, and in *caves* (wine cellars) vintners are always happy to sell a few bottles but they are often keener for you to discuss last year's vintage.

Eye-catching display

Each itinerary in this book notes the characteristic product of a region or town, and suggests a place to buy it; *calissons* (a confection of fruit and almonds) in Aix-en-Provence, wine in Gigondas, ceramics in Salernes, olive oil in Les Alpilles. The excellent shops of Avignon are only briefly mentioned in passing, there being more important items on the menu that day. A morning among the splendid architecture of the streets and squares of Aix-en-Provence is a shopping trip with an unusual cultural dimension.

Markets

Markets *(see page 69)* are the life-blood of the small producer and a significant factor in the local economies in Provence. They are also important social occasions, when people come in from the sur-

Market produce in Uzès

rounding countyside to review the progress of the *primeurs* and to bemoan the mistral, perhaps drink an *apéritif* or just chat.

Most villages have a weekly market that takes place through the year, on a day that is as fixed as the traffic jam on the *autoroute du soleil* on the first weekend in August. The stall holders will be local producers of fruit and vegetables, chickens and eggs, honey and *chèvre* (goat's cheese); garlic and olive merchants (the latter often having as many as 30 types of olives, such as *noires aux herbes, farcies aux anchois, cassées pimentées* and *nyons*); herbalists and the travelling *bouchers* (butchers) and general tradespeople who move within the sphere of local markets.

There are also the great regional markets which stallholders travel considerable distances to reach. These include the Saturday

ouleiado to take home

market in the town of Arles and the markets of L'Isle-sur-la-Sorgue, Apt and Vaison-la-Romaine. In addition to all the agricultural produce for sale you can find brightly coloured Provençal cloths and *faïence* (glazed earthenware).

The markets are the clearest indication of the relative wealth and resources of each area. You will notice, for example, how the super-abundant cheapness of fruits and vegetables in the markets of the Bouches-du-Rhône diminishes as you travel into the Var.

Souleiado

The 300-year-old Provençal tradition of hand-printing fabrics is still carried on

by one remaining firm, that of Souleiado in Tarascon. Many of the prints are Indian in origin, brought to France at the end of the 17th century to decorate the court of Louis XIV, *le roi soleil*. The colours of the fabrics are derived from the hues of Provence, notably ochres, yellows, blues and greens.

The Souleiado name gained international renown during the 1950s, when Pablo Picasso and the writer/artist Jean Cocteau adopted their shirts. Nowadays, it has the cachet (and prices) of a name such as Hermès. Souleiado has shops in all the main towns and even in some of the smaller, wealthier ones, such as Gordes.

Although the Souleiado designs and colours are indisputably magnificent, similar designs are mass produced and available at much lower prices. Larger markets have stalls selling these fabrics by the metre. Souleiado patterns can be seen all over Provence, on upholstery, tableware and as clothes.

Faïence in Provence

The art of shaping and baking clay has been known in Provence since the Middle Ages and has developed in a number of ways. One of the most sophisticated is *faïence*, the polychrome decoration of clay plates and bowls. Since the 17th century the potters of Moustiers-Sainte-Marie have had a reputation for being masters of this craft. You will find their work and that of other *faïenciers* sold across Provence. Other products of this tradition are the tiles and ceramics of Salernes and the *santons* (clay figures), sold in many pottery shops but bought ideally from a small *atelier*, such as the one on the road from St-Rémy to Les Baux.

Wine

Visiting private estates and farms to taste and purchase wines is not normally categorised as shopping, probably because it is much too pleasurable. However, there are many excellent wines to buy across Provence, particularly in the viticultural region of the southern Rhône. A good bottle of wine is one of the most potent reminders of Provence you can have in your shopping bag.

Market day in Apt

Markets

The following is a partial list of market days across the region. Trips to smaller towns, in particular, tend be enriched if they coincide with market day. Go early, as markets are almost always held in the mornings.

Every day
Marseille-Noailles
Aix-en-Provence (Place Richelme)
Avignon

Sunday
L'Isle-sur-la-Sorgue
Ramatuelle
Salernes

Monday
Bédoin
Carpentras
Saintes-Maries-de-la-Mer

Tuesday
Aix-en-Provence
Cotignac
Gordes
St-Tropez
Vaison-la-Romaine

Wednesday
Arles
Aups
Cassis
Roussillon
Sault
St-Rémy
Salernes

Thursday
Ramatuelle
Roussillon

Friday
Bonnieux
Carpentras
Cassis
Saintes-Maries-de-la-Mer

Saturday
Aix-en-Provence
(Place des Prêcheurs)
Apt
Arles
Aups
St-Tropez
Uzès

More than just vegetables

Eating Out

What is classic Provençal cuisine? As with all questions of this type regarding definitions of Provence it is hard to answer because the pages of the Provençal cookbook bear the same polyglot imprint as the rest of the culture. It is the cooking of a fairly impoverished region enriched by ingredients from the surrounding Mediterranean cultures: pasta, polenta, *soupe au pistou* (a kind of clear vegetable soup with the Provençal version of pesto added) from Italy; *crudités* and small vegetable appetisers from Spain; and *couscous* and *merguez* (spiced sausages) from North Africa.

The essential elements of Provençal cooking can be summed up as the use of olive oil, the dominance of vegetables, except in winter, when the spoils of the *chasse* – small birds, rabbits and wild boar – dominate the table, and the use of herbs and garlic for seasoning. The latter is far less common than is supposed and I doubt if anyone would now suffer the fate of Smollett: 'I was almost poisoned with garlic, which they mix in all their ragouts, and all their sauces; nay, the smell of it perfumes the very chambers, as well as every person you approach.'

At its best Provençal cooking is a natural and seasonal cuisine, retaining the taste and texture of simple, fresh ingredients from the

countryside and the sea. This was probably quite a revelation when Provence was first 'discovered'. Even in the 1950s cooking was generally much heavier, with a greater reliance on sauces, as fresh ingredients were harder to come by. As a result, the

Provençal fare

simple country cooking of a poor region was accorded an almost mythical status and exaggerated claims were made in its favour.

A good example of this is the *aïoli*. *Aïoli* is a garlic mayonnaise that usually accompanies a plate of cooked vegetables, always potato, carrots and beans, served with a piece of cod and perhaps some snails and a hard-boiled egg. Now this was clearly designed as a poor man's dish. The cod was used because it retains its freshness longer

than other fish, but by the time it reached the back country of Provence the pungent garlic sauce was probably essential. The vegetables would be leftovers from other meals.

Eating out – and outside – is one of the great pleasures of Provence. I have given it generous coverage in the itineraries and I

Seafood special

make a number of recommendations at the end of each section. Generally the restaurants I favour are those with menus reflecting what is seasonally and locally available. The most common regional dishes are listed in the *Menu Decoder* in this section *(see page 73)*.

Breakfast in Provence typically features a coffee and perhaps a *croissant, pain au chocolat* or a *brioche aux raisins*. As a rule, outside the main towns this area of the *boulanger*'s art is neglected in Provence and the pastries are often not very inspiring. If you find this to be the case, by mid-morning you will need a *casse-croûte* (literally to break the crust), otherwise known as a snack. Many cafés have a menu of *casse-croûte* and this is an area in which the *boulangers* of Provence excel. The *roulot saucisson* is a very distant relation of the pink sausage meat wrapped in stodgy pastry that passes for a sausage roll in England.

Pizza maker

71

Ideal for 'casse croûte'

Lunch in France is usually taken from noon–2pm; restaurateurs will rarely want to serve you after 2pm, although those in the coastal areas prove exception to this rule in summer. The best value and often the best meal is the fixed menu, which sometimes includes a quarter-litre of wine, which is the French working-man's lunch (the *menu fixe* or *formule*). Usually it is no more than *correct* (right for the price), but occasionally there will be an excellent local speciality. This type of meal finds its apotheosis at the Bistrot du Paradou east of Arles *(see page 75)*.

The evening should begin at 6pm with the *apéritif*, a glass of white wine in Beaumes-de-Venise but more usually a *pastis*, a blend of aromatic plants and spices slowly macerated in alcohol and aniseed essence. Each brand is marked by its own personality: Ricard and Casanis have a taste of liquorice, Pastis 51 and Pernod tend towards aniseed. Look out also for Henri Bardouin, it has an extraordinary finesse. Remember to dilute *pastis* with plenty of water.

One pastis and your stomach will be ideally prepared for eating, two or three and the bar will remain your habitat for the evening. Dinner usually begins at 8pm and you will rarely be served after 10pm, particularly in the countryside, so plan your evening accordingly.

Another day, another bottle…

I have never eaten a meal in Provence without drinking a bottle of wine – not necessarily all of it myself. I recommend that you drink the local wine. Much of the *département* of the Vaucluse is in the viticultural region of the Côte du Rhône, and has some of the most famous appellations in France: Gigondas, Châteauneuf-du-Pape, Beaumes-de-Venise (the wines from these appellations are referred to in some wine lists as the Côtes du Rhône Méridionales as opposed to the Septentrionales of the northern Rhône). Here you will be able to drink very well and relatively inexpensively. The appellations of Provence begin below Avignon and continue over a vast area of the Bouches-du-Rhône and the Var (there is also a small appellation behind Nice called Bellet). Thirty years ago good wines were difficult to find outside the small appellations of Bandol, Cassis and Palette, but nowadays they can be found all over the region. Good to great red wines in the Côteaux d'Aix-en-Provence, marvellous rosés and even some white wines in the coastal areas of the Côtes de Provence appellation. My only complaint about these wines is that they are sometimes overpriced.

Where to Eat

The restaurants below follow the regions of the main itineraries in this book, and many are mentioned in the text. Price categories are based on how much a *menu* (typically a set three-course meal with bread) will cost.

Inexpensive: *menus* up to €25; **moderate**: *menus* between €25 and €50; **expensive**: *menus* above €50.

Menu Decoder – Provençal Specialities

aïoli: garlic mayonnaise served with cooked vegetables and cod.

anchoïade: a purée of anchovies, olive oil and capers.

boeuf en daube: beef marinated in red wine and then cooked in olive oil with bacon, onions, garlic and orange zest.

bouillabaisse: a rich fish soup/stew made with a wide variety of fish (at least 5) and saffron.

bourride: same genre as above but with white fish and served with garlic.

grenouilles à la Provençale: frogs' legs, coated with flour and grilled in olive oil with garlic.

lapin à la Provençale: rabbit cooked slowly in white wine, with garlic, mustard, herbs and carrots.

loup au fenouil: sea bass grilled with fennel.

pieds-paquets: packets of tripe cooked very slowly in white wine with onions and carrots.

soupe au pistou: vegetable soup with a base of basil and garlic crushed in olive oil.

tapenade: purée of black olives, anchovy and olive oil.

The Vaucluse

Séguret

RESTAURANT LE MESCLUN
Tel: 04 90 46 93 43
A gastronomic treat. Booking essential. Closed Mondays. Moderate.

Bédoin

LE MAS DES VIGNES
Tel: 04 90 65 63 91
This place offers good-quality local cooking and some wonderful views over the Dentelles de Montmirail. Moderate.

Gigondas

HOTELLERIE 'LES FLORETS'
Tel: 04 90 65 85 01
Located 2km (1 mile) from Gigondas in the foothills of the Dentelles. Lovely restaurant with terrace for outdoor dining. Moderate.

RESTAURANT L'OUSTALET
Tel: 04 90 65 85 30
In the centre of Gigondas. Traditional Provençal cooking, first-rate wine list. Moderate.

Suzette

LES COQUELICOTS
Tel: 04 90 65 06 94
Excellent Provençal cuisine and lovely view of the Dentelles. Closed Wed. Inexpensive–Moderate.

Vaison-la-Romaine

LE BATELEUR
1 Place Théodore Aubanel
Tel: 04 90 36 28 04
A friendly restaurant beside the river specialising in contemporary regional cuisine. Closed Mon. Moderate.

Avignon

CHRISTIAN ETIENNE
10 Rue de Mons
Tel: 04 90 86 16 50
Michelin-starred chef takes classic Provençal ingredients to new heights. There is a tomato-themed *menu* and a variety of regional classics. Expensive.

LA FOURCHETTE
17 Rue Racine
Tel: 04 90 85 20 93
Atmospheric bistro-style restaurant, run by the renowned Hiély family. Busy at lunchtime. Moderate.

L'EMPREINTE
33 Rue des Teinturiers
Tel: 04 32 76 31 84
Lovely North African restaurant/tea room/art gallery, serving copious helpings of delicately spiced dishes. Jazz music at night. Inexpensive.

COMPAGNIE DES COMPTOIRS
83 Rue Joseph Vernet
Tel: 04 90 85 99 04

Terrific food in a stylish setting. Choose from modern Provençal classics or exquisite fusion food with African, Asian and Middle Eastern touches. Reasonable prices for the level of quality. Closed Sun–Mon. Moderate.

Châteauneuf-du-Pape

LA GARBURE
3 Rue Joseph-Ducos
Tel: 04 90 83 75 08
Centrally located with good local cuisine and accommodation in several cosy rooms. Inexpensive–Moderate.

MERE GERMAINE
3 Rue du Commandant Lemaître
Tel: 04 90 83 54 37
Colourful bar and brasserie, offering splendid views and good local wines. Inexpensive–Moderate.

MULE DU PAPE
2 Rue de la République
Tel: 04 90 83 79 22
Delightful brasserie and long-time local institution. Inexpensive.

Arles

BRASSERIE DE NORD-PINUS
Place du Forum

Tel: 90 93 44 44 (hotel) or
04 90 93 02 32
Attached to the famous hotel of the same name, this highly regarded brasserie on the square is decorated in 1950s style, and offers sophisticated regional cuisine. Moderate.

LE CILANTRO
31 Rue de la Porte de Laure
Tel: 04 90 18 25 05
Traditional cuisine meets world food – classic dishes are given exotic touches from Asia and elsewhere. Moderate.

JARDIN DE FRÉDÉRIC
8 Boulevard Gambetta
Tel: 04 90 92 27 76
Provençal menus in a sweet little *auberge* on main boulevard. Moderate.

Aix-en-Provence

CLOS DE LA VIOLETTE
10 Avenue de la Violette
Tel: 04 42 23 30 71
Considered the top restaurant in Aix. The chef Jean-Marc Banzo studied with Daniele Hiély in Avignon. The garden is a lovely, comfortable place to eat in the evening. Closed Sun. Booking essential in July. Expensive.

COTÉ COUR
19 Cours Mirabeau
Tel: 04 42 93 12 51
A beautifully designed, fashionable restaurant. Classic Provençal cooking accompanied by an interesting wine list. Moderate.

Marseille

MIRAMAR
12 Quai Port
Tel: 04 91 91 10 40

Les Baux

OUSTAU DE BAUMANIERE
Tel: 04 90 54 33 07
This is one of France's most famous restaurants as well as a luxury hotel. Superb Provençal cuisine. Expensive.

Maussane-les-Alpilles

BISTROT DU PARADOU
Paradou
Tel: 04 90 54 32 70
Tiny village bistro with a big reputation for its food, especially the vegetable *aïoli*. One *menu* only. Moderate.

St-Rémy

LE RESTAURANT DES ARTS
30 Boulevard Victor Hugo
Tel: 04 90 92 08 50
This is a favourite local gathering place. Moderate.

Make your reservations early

A Marseille institution set right on the old port and *the* place to sample *bouillabaisse*. Closed Sun–Mon. Expensive.

L'EPUISETTE
Vallon des Auffes
Tel: 04 91 52 17 82
Perched high up on the rocky Vallon des Auffes, this restaurant offers impressive views and excellent Provençal cuisine. Expensive.

CHEZ VINCENT
25 Rue Glandevès
Tel: 04 91 33 96 78

Special at Marseille's Miramar

Popular *trattoria* in the old port. No credit cards. Closed Mon. Inexpensive.

Along the Coast

Cassis

RESTAURANT PANISSE
4 Place Mirabeau
Tel: 04 42 01 93 93

A roadside stop

Locally caught fish and delighful views over the harbour. Inexpensive.

St-Tropez

LA PESQUIERE
1 Rue des Remparts
Tel: 04 94 97 05 92
Excellent traditional fish dishes served. Moderate.

LE SPOON BYBLOS
Hôtel Byblos
Avenue Paul Signac
Tel: 04 94 56 68 20
Choose between formal and informal food and decor at Alain Ducasse's high-concept restaurant. Expensive.

LE BISTROT
3 Place des Lices
Tel: 04 94 97 11 33
Hip brasserie serving good classic French cuisine. Moderate–Expensive.

LA BOUILLABAISSE
Plage de la Bouillabaisse
Tel: 04 94 97 54 00
Beach terrace restaurant for fresh salads and light meals; order *bouillabaisse* a day in advance. Moderate.

The Var

Cotignac

LE CLOS DES VIGNES
Route de Montfort sur Argens

Tel: 04 94 04 72 19
Gourmet restaurant in the middle of a vineyard. Beautiful setting, lovely terrace, great food. Moderate.

Aups

LES GOURMETS
5 Rue Voltaire
Tel: 04 94 70 14 97
Excellent value at this cosy Provençal restaurant. Ideal for sampling the local truffle crop. Inexpensive.

Villecroze-les-Grottes

AUBERGE DES LAVANDES
Place du Général de Gaulle
Tel: 04 94 70 76 00
Country-style *auberge* (several rooms available) with good Provençal cooking on the menu. Inexpensive.

LE COLOMBIER
Route de Draguignan
Tel: 04 94 70 63 23
Situated a short walk from Villecroze. Classic cooking with a regional accent. Moderate.

The Luberon

Roussillon

RESTAURANT LE VAL DES FEES
Rue Richard Casteau
Tel: 04 90 05 64 99
One of the nicest restaurants in the Luberon, with a lovely terrace overlooking the Val des Fées. Good for special occasions. Moderate.

Gordes

LE BOUQUET DE BASILIC
Route de Murs
Tel: 04 90 72 06 98
Provençal cooking with Sicilian overtones in a relaxed atmosphere. Closed Thurs. Moderate.

Manosque

DOMINIQUE BUCAILLE
43 Boulevard des Tilleuils
Tel: 04 92 72 32 28
Luscious regional dishes by a noted chef. Try the local lamb. Closed Sun–Mon. Expensive.

Bonnieux

LE FOURNIL
5 Place Carnot
Tel: 04 90 75 83 62
Ideal for a leisurely meal at lunch time. Shady terrace with fountain. High-quality regional food. Closed Mon. Moderate.

Dessert on its way

Calendar of Special Events

FEBRUARY / MARCH

Bormes-les-Mimosa
Mid-February: Grand Mimosa Parade.
Arles
Easter weekend: *Feria* (bullfights).
Saintes-Maries-de-la-Mer
Easter weekend: equestrian and taurine contests, folk music and dance).

APRIL

Châteauneuf-du-Pape
24 April: Wine-growers' Festival.

Entertainment in Arles

Avignon
Late April, early May: Avignon Fair.

MAY

May Day: Festivals throughout Provence.
Arles
1 May: Feast of the Gardians (the Camargue cowboys).
Aups
Weekend after 8 May: Festival of St Pancras.
St-Tropez
16–18 May: *La Bravade,* commemorating the arrival of Christian martyr Torpes (St Tropez) by boat.
Saintes-Maries-de-la-Mer
24, 25 May: popular festival and pilgrimage.

JUNE

Regionwide
24 June: Feast Day of St John the Baptist, celebrated across Provence.
Tarascon
Last Sunday in June: Festival of *Tarasque*, one of Provence's best-known folkloric festivals.

Marseille
Last three weeks: Festival de Marseille (contemporary dance, music, cinema and theatre).
Beaumes de Venise
Summer Solstice Festival.

JULY

Arles
International Festival of Photography and Festival of Arles (bullfights, music, theatre).
Avignon
Last two weeks of July/first week of August: International Theatre Festival.
Vacqueyras
Wine Festival of local Côtes du Rhone Villages appellations.
Bastille Day
14 July: firework displays and festivals all over Provence.
Vaison-la-Romaine
Last two weeks: Festival of Dance.
Aix-en-Provence
Three weeks in July: Festival of Music.
Cotignac
Late July–early August: Festival de Rocher, theatre and music.
Apt
Last Sunday: Festival of St-Anne.
Gordes
Last weekend of July–first weekend of August: 'Summer Evenings in Gordes'.
La Roque d'Anthéron
Four weeks: Piano Festival.

AUGUST

Ramatuelle
First two weeks of August: Festival of Theatre and Music.
Châteauneuf-du-Pape
First weekend: Medieval Festival (banquet, music and crafts)
St-Rémy
15 August: Feria (runing of bulls, taurine competitions).

SEPTEMBER

Arles
Mid-September: Premices du Riz (the rice harvest festival).
St-Tropez
Grape-picking festival.

NOVEMBER

Avignon
Mid-November: Festival of the Côtes du Rhône *primeurs* (first wines).

DECEMBER

Les Baux
Christmas Eve: La Fête du Pastrage (Midnight Mass).
Avignon
Santon Nativity Scene; Christmas market.
Arles
Early December/early January: Salon International des Santonniers, exhibition of nativity scenes and *santons*.

PRACTICAL information

By Air

Provence has two international airports, Marseille-Provence and Nice-Côte d'Azur. Marseille-Provence, less than 20km (12 miles) from both Aix and Marseille, is convenient for the places covered in this guide.

Air France (tel, UK: 0845 084 5111; US: 1-800 237 2747; www.airfrance. com) operates flights from Paris to Nice, Marseille, Avignon and Nîmes. **British Airways** (tel, UK: 0870 850 9850; US: 1-800 247 9297; www. ba.com) flies to Nice from Heathrow, Gatwick and Manchester. **British Midland** (tel: 0870 607

0222; www.flybmi.com) fly direct to Nice from Heathrow, Durham and East Midlands and via any of these airports from Aberdeen, Belfast, Edinburgh, Glasgow, Leeds, Manchester and Dublin. Low-cost flights to Nice are operated by **Easyjet** (tel, UK: 0905 821 0905; www.easyjet.com) from Luton and Liverpool.

Both Nice-Côte d'Azur and Marseille-Provence airports operate regular buses to the main railway stations. Taxis, especially in Nice, can be expensive.

By Rail

Travelling to Provence by rail via the Channel Tunnel is a realistic option now that the TGV (*train à grande vitesse*) from Paris takes just 2hr 40 minutes to Avignon and 3hrs to Marseille. Information and reservations are available from Rail Europe (178 Piccadilly, tel: 0870 5848 848; or book online at www.raileurope.co.uk or www.sncf.fr).

Neither Aix nor Arles is on main lines, but they are linked by local lines to Marseille and Avignon respectively.

By Car

A car is essential to make the most of Provence. However, car-hire in France is expensive, so it is worth taking your own. You can do this by ferry or on Eurotunnel (tel: 08705 353 535; www.eurotunnel.com), if coming from the UK. Driving to Provence from Paris and the North involves ploughing down the *autoroute du soleil* and paying heavy tolls. To avoid the busy motorways, follow the much quieter *itinéraires bis* or plot your own route using the back roads. It will take a bit longer, but you will see more.

There are three main options to avoid to the long drive. You could book a fly/drive package from the UK. Alternatively, French Railways (www. sncf.fr) offers a good deal on its combined train/car rental bookings. Lastly, Motorail trains carry cars and motorcycles and their passengers from Paris or the Channel ports to the South. The cost is high for the vehicle, but passengers can take advantage of the various discount passes (in the UK, tel: 08702 415 415; www. frenchmotorail.com, or www.sncf.fr).

Driving

You should carry in the car at all times a full driving licence, your vehicle registration document and evidence of insurance cover. You are also required to carry a red warning triangle for breakdowns and a spare set of bulbs.

Seat belts must be worn by the driver and all passengers. Full or dipped headlights must be used at night. If you have a right-hand drive vehicle it is important either to tint headlights yellow or apply special stickers that regulate the beam.

Speed Limits

Urban areas, 50kph (37mph).
Single carriageway roads, 90kph (56mph); on wet roads 80kph/50mph.
Dual carriageway roads, 110kph (68mph); on wet roads 100kph/62mph.
Motorways, 130kph (80mph); on wet roads 110kph/68mph.
Speeding and drink-driving offences

are heavily penalised by on-the-spot fines. Radars have been installed on many roads.

TRAVEL ESSENTIALS

Visas and Passports

All persons entering France must be in possession of a valid passport. Regulations vary between countries, but most only require a visa after 3 months. If you plan to stay longer than 3 months, contact your nearest French consulate before leaving home.

When to Visit

The sun shines down on Provence for 2,500–2,800 hours every year. There are clear, sunny days at all times of the year. Sun and heat are virtually guaranteed in July and August. There is a marked change at the end of September, when a few spectacular thunderstorms race through the region and the mistral is more likely to blow.

The mistral, the famous wind of Provence, is said to blow 170 days a year in some areas, usually in autumn and winter but occasionally in spring and summer. The wind is born in the plain of Valence where cold air from the mountains is attracted by huge masses of warm air over the Mediterranean. It starts with particular gusto when a depression of warm air comes up from the southern Mediterranean. Bottled into a narrow corridor, the wind accelerates rapidly and is uncorked in the Bouches-du-Rhône, its effects felt all over the Vaucluse and the Var. The cold, fierce wind can be depressing, but it gives the sky a spectacular brilliance and brings warmer weather in its wake.

The months of November and December are likely to be fairly wet, but around Christmas time the weather is often beautifully clear, and you can sometimes eat outside at midday (nights, however, are cold). The temperature climbs from the end of March but the weather will be variable until the end of June – periods of very warm weather, interspersed with those of unsettled weather. Despite this, spring is a wonderful season in Provence: everything is blooming, the colours are fantastic, and the tourists haven't yet descended.

The itineraries in this book are geared to July and August, when Provence is *en fête*, animated by innumerable festivals. This is, however, also when it is very crowded by the coast.

Clothing

Take cool, comfortable, casual clothes in summer. Don't forget a sun hat, sunglasses, high-factor sun cream, as well as a sweater for evenings. At other times of year dress as you would for any temperate climate.

Electricity

France runs on 220V, with double, round-pin sockets. A socket adaptor is required for the British 3-pin plug. A transformer is needed for electrical goods from countries such as the US, where the current alternates at 60 cycles and not the European standard of 50 cycles.

Time

France is one hour ahead of GMT, 6 and 9 hours respectively ahead of the East and West coasts of the US.

Banks

Opening hours: Monday–Friday, 9am–noon, 2–4.30pm. Some banks are open on Saturday mornings.

Currency

The units of the currency in France is the euro (€).

Credit Cards

Credit cards have a wide but by no means universal currency in Provence. The 'market' economy is still lubricated by cash. Some wine producers and restaurants do not accept cards. Traveller's cheques are useful.

Cash Machines

In theory PIN numbers are universally recognised, though sometimes French machines fail to recognise the magnetic strips on foreign cards. The majority of cash machines in France accept Visa, Maestro, Cirrus and Plus networks.

Tipping

This is included in the bill in restaurants, hotels and cafés. Exceptional service can be rewarded with a tip, the *pourboire* (literally meaning, 'for a drink'). Porters and doormen will expect a small tip.

Business Hours

Business hours for shops are not as long as in the UK or the US: do not expect to be able to nip out for a pint of milk at 10pm. The leisurely lunch break remains sacrosanct throughout Provence and in many villages noon is even announced by a siren. In smaller towns, banks, tourist offices, museums, shops, petrol stations, post offices – almost everything, in fact – will close for two hours. In bigger towns, larger shops and museums stay open.

The basic working hours are 9am–noon and 2–6pm, although supermarkets and other shops staying open until 7.30 or 8pm do not generally reopen until 3.30pm.

The working week for commerce is usually Tuesday–Saturday; even quite large towns can be deserted on a Monday.

Public Holidays

There are 11 *jours fériés*, or public holidays, in France. These are:

1 January
Easter Monday
1 May
8 May (V-E Day)
Ascension Thursday
Whit Monday (the Monday following the seventh Sunday after Easter)
14 July (Bastille Day)
15 August (Assumption)
1 November (All Saints' Day)
11 November (Armistice Day 1918)
Christmas Day

Closed for lunch?

Hotel Crillon Le Brave

ACCOMMODATION

Hotels

The local Tourist Office *(see page 91)* can be a very useful resource if you have trouble finding accommodation. They will have lists of *gîtes* (self-catering holiday cottages), rentable for just a weekend or for periods up to several weeks, *chambres d'hôtes* (the French equivalent of bed and breakfast), and camping sites – which are very often superbly equipped.

The following list of recommendations is structured so that it follows the main sections of this guide. Price indications are based on double occupancy: Budget: under €60; Moderate: €60–130; Expensive: over €130

Breakfast is not included in the price of a room, and in many hotels is not good value, in which case it's better to find a nice café instead. During festival periods and the month of August, hotels often raise their rates dramatically. Also, many establishments close for a month or so in winter.

Vaucluse

Bédoin

HOTEL CRILLON LE BRAVE
4km (2½ miles) from Bédoin
Tel: 04 90 65 61 61
Situated in a stunning location opposite Mont-Ventoux with lovely gardens, a good restaurant and superb rooms in Provençal style. Expensive.

HOTEL-RESTAURANT L'ESCAPADE
Tel: 04 90 65 60 21
This hotel with 11 rooms welcomes pets and gets very busy in summer. Has a good restaurant that is great value, particularly the *menu du jour.* Closed winter. Budget.

HOTEL DES PINS
Chemin des Crans
Tel: 04 90 65 92 92
Delightful hotel with lovely views and a swimming pool. Moderate.

Vaison-la-Romaine

HOTEL LE BEFFROI
Tel: 04 90 36 04 71
A characterful hotel situated in the *haute ville.* As well as offering a good restaurant, it has a 17th-century *salon* with original beamed ceiling and fireplace. Moderate.

HOTEL BURRHUS
Tel: 04 90 36 00 11
Provençal-style townhouse located in the lively Place Montfort. Budget.

La Table du Comte

Séguret

HOTEL-RESTAURANT LA TABLE DU COMTAT
Tel: 04 90 46 91 49

Small and intimate, with just eight bedrooms. Superb restaurant and a perfect setting. Expensive.

Avignon

HOTEL EUROPE
12 Place Crillon
Tel: 04 90 14 76 76
This is one of Avignon's best hotels. Once a coaching inn, it is now favoured by celebrities. Conveniently situated, quiet, elegant and comfortable. Expensive.

HOTEL MIGNON
12 Rue Joseph Vernet
Tel: 04 90 82 17 30
Mignon means cute or sweet in French, and it is. Budget.

LA MIRANDE
4 Place de la Mirande
Tel: 04 90 85 93 93
What was once a Cardinal's palace is now a gorgeous hotel. Expensive.

HOTEL DE LA GARLANDE
20 Rue Galante
Tel: 04 90 80 08 85
Pretty rooms in lively Provençal colours, on a quiet street in the pedestrian zone. Moderate.

LE COLBERT
7 Rue Agricol Perdiguer
Tel: 04 90 86 20 20
On a small street facing a lovely park in the town centre. Budget–Moderate.

Collias

HOSTELLERIE LE CASTELLAS
Tel: 04 66 22 88 88
Hotel formed from several old houses centred around a shady courtyard, and is a delight to stay in. Moderate.

Arles

GRAND HOTEL NORD-PINUS
Place du Forum
Tel: 04 90 93 44 44
Luxury hotel redolent with the history and culture of Arles, particularly when its superb bar 'La Corrida' is packed with matadors and their flamboyant retinues. Great Art Deco brasserie. Expensive.

Hôtel du Forum

HOTEL D'ARLATEN
26 Rue du Sauvage
Tel: 04 90 93 56 66
The beautifully restored home of the Counts of Arlaten, just off Place du Forum. Moderate.

HOTEL DE L'AMPHITHEATRE
5–7 Rue Diderot
Tel: 04 90 96 10 30
Beautifully renovated 17th-century house with beamed ceilings, rich

colours on the walls and retro-modern furniture. Moderate.

HOTEL LE CLOITRE
16 Rue du Cloître
Tel: 04 90 96 29 50
Quiet Provençal-style hotel in a narrow street behind the Cloisters. Moderate.

HOTEL DU FORUM
Place du Forum
Tel: 04 90 93 48 95
Lacks the style of the Nord-Pinus but a comfortable hotel with the great advantage of a swimming pool in a secluded courtyard. Moderate.

HOTEL DU MUSÉE
11 Rue du Grand Prieuré
Tel: 04 90 93 88 88
A 17th-century townhouse tucked away on a quiet street, with a pretty courtyard for breakfast. Budget.

St-Rémy

MAS DES CARASSINS
1 Chemin Gaulois
Tel: 04 90 92 15 48
This is a converted farmhouse set in secluded gardens just outside St-Rémy. Expensive.

SOUS LES FIGUIERS
3 Avenue Taillandier
Tel: 04 32 60 15 40
Relaxed atmosphere of a B&B at this delightful hotel, where most rooms have a private courtyard with a fig tree. Moderate.

Aix-en-Provence

HOTEL DES AUGUSTINS
3 Rue de la Masse
Tel: 04 42 27 28 59
Impressive hotel set in an old convent. Rooms have stone walls and stained glass; two of them have private terraces; no restaurant. Expensive.

HOTEL EN VILLE
2 Place Bellegarde
Tel: 04 42 63 34 16
Modern, stylish rooms in muted colours, with minimalist decor. Some balconies with views. Moderate.

LE MANOIR
8 Rue d'Entrecasteaux
Tel: 04 42 26 27 20
Comfortable old-style hotel, breakfast in the 14th-century cloister. Moderate.

LE PIGONNET
5 Avenue du Pigonnet
Tel: 04 42 59 02 90
Luxurious old country house-hotel, in a park in the middle of Aix. Expensive.

HOTEL DES QUATRE DAUPHINS
54 Rue Roux Alphéran
Tel: 04 42 38 16 39
In the Mazarin quarter, near the fountain of the same name. Cramped but convenient. Moderate.

Along the Coast
Cassis

HOTEL-RESTAURANT LE JARDIN D'EMILE
23 Avenue Amiral Ganteaume
Tel: 04 42 01 80 55
Located in a gorgeous tropical garden on the Plage du Bestouan. Great restaurant. Expensive.

Cassis also has a good campsite, around 10-minutes' walk from the sea, which is open mid-March to mid-November: Les Cigales, Route de Marseille; tel: 04 42 01 07 34.

Bormes-les-Mimosas

LE GRAND HOTEL
167 Route de Baguier
Tel: 04 94 71 23 72
Old-style hotel in a garden of palms overlooking the village. Budget–Moderate.

MIRAGE
38 Rue de la Vue des Iles
Tel: 04 94 05 32 60
Elegant hotel with a pool and great views out to the islands. Expensive.

Iles d'Hyeres/Porquerolles

LES GLYCINES
Place d'Armes
Tel: 04 94 58 30 36
Delightful Provençal-style hotel with a good-value restaurant. Expensive.

Gassin

HOTEL RESTAURANT BELLO VISTO
Place des Barrys
Tel: 04 94 56 17 30
A lovely hotel with a good restaurant, offering views across the Gulf of St Tropez. Budget–Moderate.

St-Tropez

It is essential to book your accommodation here well in advance.

LOU CAGNARD
18 Avenue P Roussel
Tel: 04 94 97 04 24
This place is in a more peaceful position than those listed below, towards the rear of the town and behind the Place des Lices. Closed Nov–Dec. Moderate.

HOTEL DE LA PONCHE
3 Rue des Remparts
Tel: 04 94 97 02 53

This hotel is formed from several old fishermen's cottages. Exquisitely furnished. Closed Nov–Feb. Expensive.

LE PRE DE LA MER
Route des Salins
Tel: 04 94 97 12 23
Pretty Provençal hotel just outside town; some rooms have kitchenettes. Expensive.

The Var
Salernes

LE RELAIS DE LA BELLE EPOQUE
20 Rue J. J. Rousseau
Tel: 04 94 70 60 30
This modest hotel has recently been entirely renovated. Its restaurant has a good reputation in the surrounding area. Budget.

Villecroze

AU BIEN-ETRE
Quartier des Cadenières
Tel: 04 94 70 67 57
Bien-être means 'well-being', and this quiet country hotel does its best to live up to its name. Terrace, pool and good restaurant. Budget.

Aups

AUBERGE DE LA TOUR
Rue J. P. Aloisi
Tel: 04 94 70 00 30
Probably the smartest spot in the town. The restaurant does good pizzas. Budget.

GRAND HOTEL
Place Gendarme-Duchâtel
Tel: 04 94 70 10 82
Friendly, *correct* hotel with a good restaurant. Budget.

LE PROVENÇAL
Place Bidouret
Tel: 04 94 70 00 24
Small, rustic hotel. Budget.

Tourtour

BASTIDE DE TOURTOUR
Tel: 04 98 10 54 20
Luxury hotel in its own park with pool and restaurant. Expensive.

LA PETITE AUBERGE
1km (½ mile) south of the village on the D77
Tel: 04 98 10 26 16
With great views, a swimming pool and a good restaurant, this is something special. Moderate.

The Luberon
Apt

AUBERGE DU LUBERON
17 Quai Léon-Sagy
Tel: 04 90 74 12 50
The best hotel in Apt, just across the river from the Place de la Bouquerie. Good restaurant. Moderate.

HOTEL LE PALAIS
Place Gabriel Péri
Tel: 04 90 04 89 32
Good cheap rooms in the middle of town. Closed mid-Nov to mid-Mar. Budget.

Roussillon

HOTEL REVES DES OCRES
Route de Gordes
Tel: 04 90 05 60 50
The only hotel in the village – with remarkably reasonable prices. Some rooms have balconies with good views. Moderate.

Murs

MAS DU LORIOT
Route de Joucas (D1024)
Tel: 04 90 72 62 62
Lost in the hills about 5km (3 miles) from Roussillon, this intimate hotel has eight airy, tastefully furnished rooms, each with a balcony and lovely view across the Luberon countryside. Closed Dec–Feb. Moderate.

Gordes

LA BASTIDE DE GORDES
Route de Combe
Tel: 04 90 72 12 12
Smart hotel and spa on the town walls with splendid views of surrounding country. Expensive.

LES BORIES
On the D177 to Sénanque
Tel: 04 90 72 00 51
Part of the restaurant of this elegant hotel and spa is in a *borie (see page 62)* but, make no mistake, this is a luxury hotel. Expensive.

AUBERGE DE CARCARILLE
2km east of Gordes on the D2
Tel: 04 90 72 02 63
The Auberge de Carcarille, which has its own swimming pool, is set in the countryside, so you'll probably need a car to get here. The restaurant is good value. Moderate.

Bonnieux

HOTEL CÉSAR
Place de la Liberté
Tel: 04 90 75 96 35
The dining room at this hotel looks out over the valley to Lacoste, which is delightful. Budget.

NIGHTLIFE

Come meet me in some dead café –
A puff of cognac or a sip of smoke.
(from *Avignon* by Lawrence Durrell)

Nightlife in Provence is sitting in the Place du Forum in Arles listening to a saxophone and bass improvise around the chords of *Round Midnight;* it is ordering just one last bottle of rosé with the patron yawning; it is the village ball and *fête*. It might be drinking a coffee or promenading on the Cours Mirabeau, or listening to the string quartet on the terrace of a

Nightlife coming to the Place du Forum, Arles

château. It is occasionally an open-air film, the festival of theatre in Avignon, classical music in Aix or jazz in Hyères. It can be the nightclub, but that is really the preserve of the coast and above all St-Tropez, and it disappears completely in winter.

The best guides to what is on are the local newspapers.

HEALTH & EMERGENCIES

The number for the emergency services (SAMU) is 15.

France has excellent health care. The patient pays costs up front and 75–80 percent of these are later reimbursed. Citizens of the EU are entitled to health care in France on the same terms as the French; that is, payment in advance followed by reimbursement from their own government. To take advantage of this system, British citizens need to carry a European Health Insurance Card (tel: 0845 606 2030, www.dh.gov.uk, or obtain an application form from the post office).

Refunds extend to any medicines prescribed by the doctor. Be aware that doctors in France prescribe very freely and the cost of medicines can add up (though Americans will still be astonished at how cheap they are). It is always advisable to take out private medical insurance before travelling.

A pharmacist has considerable powers to prescribe medicine so for minor problems consult one before visiting a doctor. Avoid buying your toiletries at the pharmacy: they are much cheaper at the supermarket.

Police and Crime

The number for an emergency is 17.

Petty theft is inevitably a problem in the bigger towns and on the coast, although less so in rural areas. CD players and luggage in cars are the usual targets. Thefts should be reported to the local *gendarmerie* (police station), where you will be issued with the necessary papers to make an insurance claim. A tip: don't go at lunch time.

Fires

The number for an emergency is 18.

Forest fires are a perennial problem in Provence, and fire fighting equipment is in place in every *commune*. Devastation every year is severe; the heavily forested Var *département* suffers most.

Cooking on an open fire in the forest and while *camping sauvage* (on outside designated sites) are both forbid-

Guardians of the law in Aix

country's international call number. These can be found in the front of the *Pages Jaunes* section of the telephone directory *(annuaire)* or on the information section in a telephone box.

If using a US credit phone card, call the company's access number: AT&T, 0800-99-00-11; MCI, 0800-99-00-19; Sprint, 0800-99-00-87.

Public Phones

Public phones operate with cards. The cards with a chip *(cartes à puce)* work only in pay phones, while those with a code *(cartes à code)* work with any phone (and generally offer cheaper rates than the phone companies). Phonecards are available from post offices, stationers, railway stations, some cafés and *tabacs*.

den in Provence, and infringements are heavily penalised. You should be very careful with cigarette ends, etc.

POST

Most post offices open from 9am–noon and 2–6 or 7pm, Monday to Friday and 9am–noon on Saturday. Stamps *(timbres)* can also be bought from tobacconists *(tabacs)*, which can be found in many bars, although for letters with destinations outside the EU you will need to go to the post office.

TELEPHONES

Telephone numbers in France have ten digits, which are always written in sets of two, e.g. 04 23 45 67 89 (04 is the code for Provence). To telephone France from abroad, omit the initial zero. The cheapest times to telephone are weekdays 7pm–8am and at weekends.

International calls

To make an international call from Provence, dial 00 followed by the

MEDIA

Regional and provincial papers account for over two-thirds of the daily sale, a pattern similar to the US. Newspapers such as *Le Provençal* and *Var Matin* have only a few pages of hard news but are excellent sources of local information of all kinds. On the coast, look out for *The Riviera Reporter*, a local magazine for the expat community.

INFORMATION & MAPS

The itineraries in this guide have been traced on the pull-out map in the wallet at the back of this book. Other good maps of the region include Michelin map No. 245, in the series 1cm: 2km (coloured yellow), or map No. R18 in the *Institut Géographique National* red series, 1cm: 2½km.

Local tourist offices are good sources for town plans and local maps, and for information regarding opening hours of museums and other local attractions, as well as restaurants.

In the Vaucluse such tourist offices are very strong on publicising outdoor activities and they usually sell maps and guides specifically designed for walkers and cyclists.

LANGUAGE

The curiosity of the French language in Provence is the accent. Many words finish with a kind of clanging sound. Remember that social contacts are more formal in France than in many countries – witness the shaking of hands and the ritual of the *bise* (kiss).

Here are a few useful phrases:

Good morning/hello *Bonjour*
Good evening *Bonsoir*
How are you? *Comment allez-vous?*
I'm well *Très bien, merci*
Goodbye *Au revoir*
Please *S'il vous plaît*
Thank you *Merci*
You are welcome *Je vous en prie*
Enjoy your meal *Bon appétit*
See you later *A tout à l'heure*

USEFUL ADDRESSES

Tourist Offices

Aix-en-Provence: 2 Place du Général de Gaulle, 13100 Aix-en-Provence. Tel: 04 42 16 11 61.
Apt: 20 Avenue Philippe de Gérard, 84400 Apt. Tel: 04 90 74 03 18.
Arles: Boulevard des Lices, 13200 Arles. Tel: 04 90 18 41 20.

Avignon: 41 Cours Jean Jaurès, 84000 Avignon. Tel: 04 32 74 32 74.
Aups: Place Frédéric Mistral, 83630 Aups. Tel: 04 94 84 00 69.
Cassis: Quai des Moulins, 13260 Cassis. Tel: 08 92 25 98 92.
Saintes-Maries-de-la-Mer, 5 Avenue Van Gogh. Tel: 04 90 97 82 55.
Salernes: Place Gabriel Péri, 83690 Salernes. Tel: 04 94 70 69 02.
St-Tropez: Quai Jean Jaurès, 83990 St-Tropez. Tel: 04 94 97 45 21.
Vaison-la-Romaine: Place du Chanoine Sautel, 84110 Vaison. Tel: 04 90 36 02 11.
London: French Tourist Office, 178 Piccadilly, London W1J 9AL. Tel: 09068 244123. www.franceguide.com
New York: French Tourist Office, 444 Madison Avenue, New York, NY 10022. Tel: 410 286 8310.
A complete list of tourist offices is available at www.tourisme.fr.

FURTHER READING

Travels Through France and Italy by Tobias Smollett, Oxford's World's Classics.
Hills and the Sea by Hilaire Belloc, Greenwood Press.
Letters from My Windmill by Alphonse Daudet, Penguin Classics.
Petrarch and his World by Morris Bishop, Chatto & Windus.
The Waning of the Middle Ages by J Huizinga, Penguin (classic study, good on the Courts of Love).
Provence: from Minstrels to the Machine by Ford Madox Ford, WW Norton.
Travels in the South of France by Stendhal. John Calder

Also by APA Publications

Insight Guide: Provence
Insight Guide: French Riviera
Insight Pocket Guide: French Riviera
Insight Compact Guide: French Riviera

Index

ACKNOWLEDGMENTS

Photography **Gil Galvin and George Taylor** *and*

Page 1 **Bill Wassman**

Pages 8/9, 36B, 43, 79 **Catherine Karnow**

Production Editor **Erich Meyer**

Cover Design **Tanvir Virdee**

Cover Photography **Vidler/Prisma/age fotostock/Superstock**

(*front*)

Gil Galvin and George Taylor *(back)*

Cartography **Berndtson & Berndtson**